SO-FQW-549

Seeds Of Wisdom

Jesus, The Author And Finisher Of My Faith

Lena Schepis

Seeds
Of
Wisdom

*Jesus, The Author And
Finisher Of My Faith*

Lena Schepis

Copyright © 2003
All Rights Reserved

PUBLISHED BY:
BRENTWOOD CHRISTIAN PRESS
4000 BEALLWOOD AVENUE
COLUMBUS, GEORGIA 31904

DEDICATION

Above and first of all I dedicate this book to our **MIGHTY GOD** - whose Holy Spirit spoke the words contained in this book, for HE IS THE REAL AUTHOR! Praise the Lord!

Second - I would like to express my love and gratitude to Rev. Ann Sandell of the Lovepower Music & Miracles Ministries in Minneapolis, Mn. She was the first spiritual "mother" God gave to me. Through her and the many people in her church, I learned the real agapé love of God! I learned how important it is to reach out to God's people and tell them of "THE GOSPEL OF GOOD NEWS", just like our LORD JESUS OF NAZARETH did. I would also like to say to Pastor David Klefsaas from Rejoice Church in Savage, Mn. thank you from the depth of my heart! When you taught this young Christian the beauty of worshipping our Lord with all of our hearts, no matter what the circumstances are in our lives. For the people in Rejoice - thank you for seeing me through the many battles that our spiritual enemy has launched against me.

I would like to express my deep love, gratitude, and respect to Pastor Edward and his wife Martha Zaremba of the Assembly of God church in Belleville, NJ. You have showed me how to persevere no matter what should happen in my life! You taught me how to be obedient to our LORD'S WILL AND DIRECTION". You have encouraged me, you have stood in the "gap" for me and my family. You taught me the power of prayer when it is "straight" from our hearts - "TO THE FATHER'S HEART"!

To Rev. Margarita Guzman at Gospel Light Prison Ministry in Newark, NJ - your love and acceptance of God's people no matter from what nation they have originated from and most of all - inviting me to give my miracle testimony on my 10th christian "birthday - Oct. 28, 1999. I now understand the enormous risk you took in allowing me to glorify our awesome God. Thank you so very much for by your example, you encouraged me to be bold to speak and do the work - "THE LABOR OF LOVE" - God has called me to do in these end times. I pray God's blessing and favor upon you and all of your church members.

I would like to thank Pastor - Rev. Anthony S. Ventola and his leadership team at Agapé Worship Center in Bloomfield, NJ. When my Holy Spirit brought me to his door-step, he and his leadership have taught me to live a life pleasing to our God. Here I "saw" and grew spiritually in the total abandonment of God's Holy Sovereign will. 'Thank you for your prayers, support and teaching this young Christian how to be a servant - 1st to our Lord, 2nd to one another. Pastor Ventola, as you spoke from the depth of your spirit - I too pray that our God will "show off" with this book! To my present pastor - Rev. John and his wife Donna Esposito and to Rev. Danny and to all in Christian Faith Center in Bloomfield, NJ - thank you for your warm welcome, prayers and friendship. Pastor John, ever since I have stepped into your church, our Lord has been confirming His will to be your student. I am enjoying the "points" you bring out in the scriptures.

ACKNOWLEDGEMENT

I would like to mention that in these thirteen years God has turned me around 360° - that is from Hell to God's joyful kingdom, I have met and been blessed by so many Christians who have become so very dear to my heart - Bernice in Eden Prairie, Mn. who has opened her home to me when I did not have a place to stay, and for being my prayer partner; For Annamarie Jabs and her family, when I first came to Minnesota, you have adopted me and my son and helped us to survive the first brutal cold winter, to Christine, Valerie, and to so many countless more to include in on this page - Thank you from the depths of me for your prayers, encouragement, holding on to me when our spiritual enemy of our souls roared in my life, by not letting me slip back into darkness. For the many "prophetic" words spoken over me over these many years here in NJ and in Mn. in which it only proves that the messages were from my Abba Father to keep me on the path He set me on. To my dearly loved friends, Edwin & Carmen Cordero of Agapé Worship Center in Bloomfield, NJ, thank you for your time in typing, editing this book. For your prayers, for your shoulders when the tears wouldn't stop flowing. God has and always will be faithful in providing me with a "family" to hold me close to Him. Praise God!

To my sister, Mary, I thank God for you, even though our lives were so different, and at times we were enemies, in these past years my prayers for this family to be healed and restored is coming to pass. Thank you for being my strength in my weak times, my sounding board when life was to wild and crazy, for listening to me when God spoke to us. For being my prayer partner. God really has and is moving in and through us! I love you so very much for your patience with me. I really thank God for you!

To my brother, Nick - I thank you so very much for the countless times you have tried to "rescue this nut from hell"! To Elaine, my sister-in-law, thanks for having patience and understanding and visiting me when I was a patient in the "nutty ward". I love and miss you both so very much! To my niece and nephew - Tracy and Ezra I pray that you will read this book and get to really know the only God of our faith. I love you both very much and I pray that you will grow up to be Godly men and women of faith. To my niece Evana, thank you so very much for giving me "gifts" for this book to become a reality. To Roseanna - my prayer is only that you give God a place in your heart and let Him heal you of the wounds the real "enemy" has inflicted on your very young soul.

To my mother, who truly does trust and believe in God in her own way, for her prayers! pray that I can now be a walking, talking witness of God's great infinite love and patience with us. I love you Mom! God bless and keep you in His loving arms forever!

To my only son, Michael Eric, my prayer is that you will stop hating me for the crazy past we had. And if ever you do read this book - you will stop fighting Abba Father who **really** is the one and only true Living God! You have witnessed the change in me, and you have admitted that "only God" could have done this miracle. Please, Michael, wake up before it is too late!

REMEMBER

I remember when you were born -
I was so afraid I would do something wrong -
I took you home and held you tight -
You took hold of my breast without a fight -
You learned right away the body scent and the sound of my voice!
I knew it was at that moment -
We were bound and we didn't have a choice!
You are my first born, and my son!
Remember if we work together -
Any battle can be won!

Where ever you go in life and what ever you do -
Remember, I am always with you!
Remember the scent of my body -
Remember the sound of my voice -
Remember in life you will always have a choice!

Author - anonymous

CONTENTS

	Page
INTRODUCTION	9
THE RE-BIRTH	21
THE FATHER'S LOVE	35
HIS BANNER OVER ME IS LOVE	61
LOVER OF MY SOUL	85
THE COVENANT OF LOVE, GRACE & MERCY	103
THE GREAT COMMISSION	111
OF BLESSINGS AND CURSES	133
THE BLESSED ANTICIPATION OF PROMISES KEPT	189
THE WHITE HARVEST	211
THE BRIDAL COMPANY'S HOPE	215
THE MARRIAGE FEAST	229
OF REWARDS AND JUDGMENTS	241
THE GREAT PROMISE OF THE LORD - FULFILLED	255

INTRODUCTION

SCRIPTURE: PROVERBS 9:10
(NEW KING JAMES VERSION)

"THE FEAR OF THE LORD IS THE BEGINNING OF WISDOM, AND THE KNOWLEDGE OF THE HOLY ONE IS UNDERSTANDING"!

"PRAISE THE LORD"!

By the events of these past few decades, at least from my teen years to this moment, the ever increasing waves of crime and violence is steadily rising!
Look at any TV newscast or pick-up a newspaper, and we can see the "evidence" of these times.
One can only wonder - "will this ever end"?
As a product of the post World War II generation, it would seem we are on a roller coaster ride to self-doom and destruction - all in the mighty labels such **as: "FREEDOM!"; "PURSUIT OF LIBERTY AND HAPPINESS"!; "CIVIL RIGHTS"!; WOMEN'S RIGHTS"!; "GAY RIGHTS"!; "RELIGIOUS FREEDOM"! etc., etc., etc.**
BUT -
At what cost do we achieve such lofty ideals?
The late 60's "revolution" against war, hypocrisy, and the "establishment", only brought forth a new generation of children more lost and confused than we the older generation - already were!
WHY?
All the wise men, gurus, and the "gods" of wood, stone, money, astrology, "mother nature", cannot give us peace - that is -
REAL - TANGIBLE PEACE - WITHIN US!
It's the emptiness deep inside us where we try to "fill" that aching, empty hollowness with love, fame and fortune at any

10

and all cost so we can like and live - with our ownselves! Let alone with having a deep, loving, committed relationship with anyone else!

WHY?

All the wealth and pleasure and glamour this world has and offers, cannot fill the "special" temple-house of the ONE AND ONLY TRUE CREATOR - GOD - ABBA FATHER - HE ALONE HAS CREATED US - NOT SOME FAR-FETCHED MEAN-INGLESS MUMBO JUMBO OF THE "EXULTED" SOCIETY OF SCIENTISTS! AND ONLY HE AND HE ALONE CAN "FILL" THAT HOLLOW EMPTINESS WITHIN US!

That, my friend -
Is the knowledge that there really is a **SUPREME, SOVEREIGN, MIGHTY, REAL-LIVING GOD!**
This book fashioned by the true wisdom of this one - true - *LIV-ING GOD, IS THE BEGINNING OF "FEARING THE LORD" - THAT IS - HAVING THE MIRACULOUS REVELATION THAT HE IS THE ONE AND ONLY - "GREAT I AM" SPOKEN IN WRITTEN WORDS IN AN ANCIENT BOOK - WE CALL BY SO MANY TITLES -*
YET -
IT IS ONLY - HIS WORDS - ALIVE - LIVING AND INTERACT-ING DEEPLY INSIDE THAT EMPTY HOLLOWNESS OF OUR SOULS,

HOW?

By allowing yourself to read this book - yes - **THE HOLY SPIRIT OF GOD** *REALLY DID WRITE ALL THE WORDS CONTAINED HERE* - though I am only a mere human being -
Yet -
What is contained in these pages is not human intelligence, nor was I educated to "creatively" write. I challenge you to pick up a few different interpretations of the Bible:
> 1. The New King James Version
> 2. The New Revised King James Version
> 3. The Amplified Daily Living Bible

Compare the words, the style, the format of those authors, the time span of the authors when their "work" was written. Now compare all those with this one...

Is the "fear" - the awesome Wisdom of God's Truth - Reality been established in your stony cold skeptical hearts?

This book testifies, "Written by the Holy Spirit of God - thru - *His servant.*

I pray to Abba Father, in the most holy precious Name of His one and only begotten Son, Jesus of Nazareth, that as you continue to read, your soul will be filled with His Love - for in these present days - gone is the "FEAR" OF THE LORD! THAT IS - HAVING AN AWED RESPECT OF GOD!

IN THIS LAND, SO TOO, GONE IS HIS LOVE, FOR WE HAVE LOST THE GREATEST TREASURE -

HIS WISDOM!

THE PARABLE OF
THE FARMER AND THE SEED

"THE KINGDOM OF HEAVEN IS LIKE A FARMER SOWING GOOD SEED IN HIS FIELD;
"BUT ONE NIGHT AS HE SLEPT, HIS ENEMY CAME AND SOWED THISTLES AMONG THE WHEAT.
"WHEN THE CROP BEGAN TO GROW, THE THISTLES GREW TOO.
"THE FARMER'S MEN CAME AND TOLD HIM,
"SIR, THE FIELD WHERE YOU PLANTED THE CHOICE SEED IS FULL OF THISTLES!
"AN ENEMY HAS DONE IT" HE EXCLAIMED.
"SHALL WE PULL OUT THE THISTLES?" THEY ASKED.
"NO," HE REPLIED.
"YOU'LL HURT THE WHEAT IF YOU DO. LET BOTH GROW TOGETHER UNTIL THE HARVEST, AND I WILL TELL THE REAPERS TO SORT OUT THE THISTLES AND BURN THEM, AND PUT THE WHEAT IN THE BARN."
{MATTHEW 13:24-30 FROM THE LIVING BIBLE.}

THE DISCIPLES ASKED JESUS OF NAZARETH TO EXPLAIN TO THEM ILLUSTRATION OF THE THISTLES AND THE WHEAT.

"ALL RIGHT," JESUS SAID, "I AM THE FARMER WHO SOWS THE CHOICE SEED. THE FIELD IS THE WORLD, AND THE SEED REPRESENTS THE PEOPLE OF THE KINGDOM; THE THISTLES ARE THE PEOPLE BELONG-ING TO SATAN. THE ENEMY WHO SOWED THE THISTLES AMONG THE WHEAT IS THE DEVIL; THE HAR-VEST IS THE END OF THE WORLD, AND THE REAPERS

ARE THE ANGELS.

"JUST AS IN THE STORY THE THISTLES ARE SEPARATED AND BURNED, SO SHALL IT BE AT THE END OF THE WORLD: I WILL SEND MY ANGELS AND THEY WILL SEPARATE OUT OF THE KINGDOM EVERY TEMPTATION AND ALL WHO ARE EVIL, AND THROW THEM INTO THE FURNACE AND BURN THEM.

"THERE SHALL BE WEEPING GNASHING OF TEETH. THEN THE GODLY SHALL SHINE AS THE SUN IN THEIR FATHER'S KINGDOM. LET THOSE WITH EARS, LISTEN!"

{MATTHEW 13:36-43 FROM THE LIVING BIBLE}

PROVERBS 9:9 - 10

"TEACH A WISE MAN, AND HE WILL BE THE WISER"
"TEACH A GOOD MAN, AND HE WILL LEARN MORE.
"**FOR THE REVERENCE AND FEAR OF GOD ARE
BASIC TO ALL WISDOM.**
"**KNOWING GOD RESULTS IN EVERY OTHER KIND
OF UNDERSTANDING**".

(From the Daily Living Bible Version. Stress underlining by
author to bring a point across more clearly to the reader. *L.*)

15

THE HIGH CALLING

IF GOD HAS CALLED YOU TO BE TRULY LIKE JESUS, HE WILL DRAW YOU INTO A LIFE OF CRUCIFIXION AND HUMILITY, AND PUT ON YOU DEMANDS OF OBEDIENCE THAT SOMETIMES WILL NOT ALLOW YOU TO FOLLOW OTHER CHRISTIANS. IN MANY WAYS HE WILL SEEM TO LET OTHER GOOD PEOPLE DO THINGS HE WILL NOT LET YOU DO.

OTHER CHRISTIANS, AN EVEN MINISTERS, WHO SEEM VERY RELIGIOUS AND USEFUL MAY PUSH THEM-SELVES, PULL STRINGS, AND WORK SCHEMES TO CARRY OUT THEIR PLANS, BUT YOU CANNOT DO THESE THINGS. AND IF YOU ATTEMPT THEM, YOU WILL MEET WITH SUCH FAILURE AND REBUKE FROM THE LORD AS TO MAKE YOU SORELY PENITENT.

OTHERS CAN BRAG ABOUT THEMSELVES, ABOUT THEIR WORK, ABOUT THEIR SUCCESS, ABOUT THEIR WRITINGS, BUT THE HOLY SPIRIT WILL NOT ALLOW YOU TO DO ANY SUCH THING; AND IF YOU BEGIN BRAGGING, HE WILL LEAD YOU INTO SOME DEEP MORTIFICATION THAT WILL MAKE YOU DESPISE YOURSELF AND ALL YOUR GOOD WORKS.

OTHERS WILL BE ALLOWED TO SUCCEED IN MAK-ING GREAT SUMS OF MONEY, OR HAVING A LEGACY LEFT TO THEM, OR IN HAVING LUXURIES, BUT GOD MAY ONLY SUPPLY YOU DAILY, BECAUSE HE WANTS YOU TO HAVE SOMETHING FAR BETTER THAN GOLD - A HELPLESS DEPENDENCE ON HIM - THAT HE MAY HAVE THE PRIVILEGE OF PROVIDING YOUR NEEDS DAILY OUT OF THE UNSEEN TREASURY.

THE LORD MAY LET OTHERS BE HONORED AND KEEP YOU HIDDEN AWAY IN OBSCURITY, BECAUSE HE WANTS TO PRODUCE SOME CHOICE, FRAGRANT FRUIT FOR HIS COMING GLORY, WHICH CAN ONLY BE PRODUCED IN THE SHADE.

GOD WILL LET OTHERS BE GREAT, BUT KEEP YOU SMALL. HE WILL LET OTHERS DO A WORK FOR HIM, AND GET THE CREDIT FOR IT, BUT HE WILL MAKE YOU WORK AND TOIL WITHOUT KNOWING HOW MUCH YOU ARE DOING. AND THEN TO MAKE YOUR WORK STILL MORE PRECIOUS, HE WILL LET OTHERS GET THE CREDIT FOR THE WORK WHICH YOU HAVE DONE, AND THIS WILL MAKE YOUR REWARD TEN TIMES GREATER WHEN JESUS COMES.

THE HOLY SPIRIT WILL PUT A STRICT WATCH ON YOU, WITH JEALOUS LOVE, AND REBUKE YOU FOR LITTLE WORDS AND FEELINGS OR FOR WASTED TIME, WHICH OTHER CHRISTIANS NEVER SEEM DISTRESSED OVER.

SO MAKE UP YOUR MIND THAT GOD IS AN INFINITE SOVEREIGN WHO HAS A RIGHT TO DO AS HE PLEASES WITH HIS OWN, AND NEEDS NOT EXPLAIN TO YOU A THOUSAND THINGS WHICH MAY PUZZLE YOUR REASON IN HIS DEALINGS WITH YOU.

GOD WILL TAKE YOU AT YOUR WORD; AND IF YOU ABSOLUTELY SELL YOURSELF TO BE HIS SLAVE, HE WILL WRAP YOU UP IN A JEALOUS LOVE AND LET OTHER PEOPLE SAY AND DO MANY THINGS YOU CANNOT DO OR SAY.

SETTLE IT FOREVER, THAT YOU ARE TO DEAL DIRECTLY WITH THE HOLY SPIRIT, AND THAT HE IS TO HAVE THE PRIVILEGE OF TYING YOUR TONGUE, OR CHAINING YOUR HAND, OR CLOSING YOUR EYES IN WAYS THAT OTHERS ARE NOT DISCIPLINED.

NOW, WHEN YOU ARE SO POSSESSED WITH THE LIVING GOD THAT YOU ARE, IN YOUR SECRET HEART

PLEASED AND DELIGHTED OVER THIS PECULIAR, PERSONAL, PRIVATE JEALOUS GUARDIANSHIP AND MANAGEMENT OF THE HOLY SPIRIT OVER YOUR LIFE, YOU WILL HAVE FOUND THE VESTIBULE OF HEAVEN.

- UNKNOWN

PROPHECY 2/24/93

OH! MY BELOVED!
HEAR MY CALL!
I AM CALLING YOU TO COME OUT OF THE TOMB!
AS I CALLED LAZARUS TO COME OUT -
SO, I CALL YOU, MY BELOVED!
COME OUT FROM THE TOMB OF YOUR PAST, OF YOUR
SINS, OF YOUR DARKNESS!

COME OUT!
BE CLOTHED IN GARMENTS OF LIFE, INSTEAD OF THE
GRAVE CLOTHS!
COME, BATHE AND REFRESH THYSELVES IN MY ATON-
ING BLOOD -
DRINK DEEPLY FROM THE LIVING WATERS OF MY
HOLY SPIRIT!
FOR I AM LIFE!
FOR I AM THE BRIGHT MORNING STAR -
DAWN IS APPROACHING -
DARKNESS FADES -
SO, COME OUT INTO THE LIGHT OF MY GLORY -
LET IT TRANSFORM YOU IN THE LIKENESS OF MY
IMAGE -
LET MY LIGHT BE YOUR LIGHT IN THE DAWNING OF
YOUR SALVATION!

THE RE-BIRTH

JOHN 3:10

TRANSFIGURATION

OUT OF THE WRECK I RISE!
"WHO SHALL SEPARATE US FROM THE LOVE OF CHRIST"? (ROMANS 8:35)
OH! GOD! ARE YOU REALLY THERE IN HEAVEN?
OH! GOD! ARE YOU REALLY HERE BESIDE ME?
MY LIFE SEEMS TO BE LIKE A FRAIL BOAT IN THE CURRENTS OF LIVING IN THIS WORLD!
OH! GOD! DO YOU STILL REMEMBER WHEN YOU WERE IN THE BOAT WITH VERY HUMAN BEINGS?
DO YOU STILL REMEMBER HOW FRIGHTENED OUT OF THEIR WITS THEY WERE WHEN THE WAVES WERE MOUNTAINS OF GRIEF?
LORD? ARE YOU ABLE TO HEAR ME THROUGH THIS TEMPEST?
LORD? ALL I CAN HEAR IS THE SCREAMING WIND!
LORD? ALL I CAN FEEL IS THIS BOAT SINKING!
LORD????!!
'BE STILL AND KNOW THAT I AM THE LORD THY GOD!'
LORD'? WAS THAT YOU THAT I HEARD?
'FEAR NOT MY BELOVED!'
'I AM ALWAYS WITH THEE!'
LORD! HELP ME! I AM A SHIP-WRECKED SOUL TOSSED IN THIS TEMPEST OF WOES!
'WHO SHALL SEPARATE US FROM THE LOVE OF CHRIST?'
'SHALL TRIBULATION?'
LORD! ARE YOU TELLING ME THAT I SHOULDN'T BE AFRAID OF THIS STORM?
'BELOVED! MY VOICE IS IN THE WIND -
'FEAR NOT!'

'SHALL ANGUISH SEPARATE US?'
LORD! I AM SO THIRSTY FOR SOME COOL SWEET WATER -
BUT ALL AROUND ME ARE BITTER WATERS -
THEY STRETCH THEIR ARMS TOWARDS ME -
SEEKING MY DESTRUCTION!
'SHALL FAMINE?'
LORD! I AM SO VERY HUNGRY FOR REAL TRUTH AND JUSTICE -
THIS WORLD IS SO VERY EVIL!
'NAY! IN ALL THESE THINGS WE ARE MORE THAN CONQUERORS THROUGH HIM THAT LOVED US!'
LORD! YOU ARE REALLY HERE BESIDE ME!
LORD! YOU REALLY DO HEAR ME!
LORD! I PRAISE YOU FOR YOUR EVERLASTING TRUSTWORTHY FAITHFULNESS TOWARDS ME -
A WRETCHED WRECK - BUT NO LONGER - FOR I AM YOURS FOREVER!

(*Footnote) In reading my book: "My Utmost For His Highest" by Oswald Chambers, today 7/27/94, beginning around 10:30 A.M., here at the hospital were I work, there are moments of intense busyness than there are moments of quietness, I hear the still small voice of my sweet Lord! Yesterday, 7/26/94, there was a confrontation with an old acquaintance from my past. Her words were like very sharp knives and she "expertly" shot each one into the barely healed wounds of my past. In a seemingly vicious tongue attack she emotionally ripped me apart by her wolf-like fang-words! But praise God that His Holy Spirit was in control! I was not emotional as I used to be! Praise the Lord! That is a miracle! God's faithfulness once again was confirmed! His promise that He would heal me of my emotions as prophesied by a visiting India pastor in Minnesota is fruitful of His glory! I hope and pray that this woman has seen the difference in me. Or hell

23

would have had another "murderous" field day on this "young" Christian! When I left her, though the inner wounds were "bleeding profusely", the tears began to flow, the pain began to be unbearable, soon without realizing it, I was slipping back into my old "nature". I was feeling sorry for myself! So here I am almost 4:00 P.M., and I'm still crying out to the Lord - "Please God - hear this wretched wreck - lift me out of this storm if possible, and if that is not your sovereign will - then please walk with me through this storm. In your most precious sweet Name - Jesus Christ of Nazareth, I pray. Thank you so very much for hearing my cry to You, My God! Amen!

I COPIED THIS FROM A BOOK CALLED: *STREAMS IN THE DESERT II*, MRS. CHARLES E. COWMAN

JANUARY 19___

AND LEAD US NOT INTO TEMPTATION.... (MATT. 6:13).

WHEN TEMPTED:
> FORGET THE SLANDER YOU HAVE HEARD,
> FORGET THE HASTY, UNKIND WORD;
> FORGET THE QUARREL AND THE CAUSE,
> FORGET THE WHOLE AFFAIR, BECAUSE,
> FORGETTING IS THE ONLY WAY.
> FORGET THE STORM OF YESTERDAY.
> FORGET THE CHAP WHOSE SOUR FACE
> FORGETS TO SMILE IN ANY PLACE.
> FORGET THAT YOU'RE NOT A MILLIONAIRE,
> FORGET THE GRAY STREAKS IN YOUR HAIR.
> FORGET THE COFFEE WHEN IT'S COLD.
> FORGET TO KICK, FORGET TO SCOLD,
> FORGET THE PLUMBER'S AWFUL CHARGE,
> FORGET THE DOCTOR'S BILL IS LARGE;
> FORGET THE REPAIR MAN AND HIS WAYS,
> FORGET THE WINTER'S BLUSTERY DAYS.
> FORGET THE NEIGHBOR'S WAGGING TONGUE.
> **BUT DON'T**
> FORGET GOD WHEN DAY IS DONE.

UNKNOWN

THE ANSWER TO YOUR HEART

HOW DO THE STARS STAY SO HIGH ABOVE?
WHERE DOES THE SUN RECEIVE HER WARMTH?
WHY DO THE OCEANS SWIRL IN TURMOIL?
WHY WE CANNOT SEE THE WIND?
WHY DO I EXIST?
WHAT IS MY PURPOSE OF EXISTING?
WHO HAS THE ANSWERS TO MY HEART'S DEEP PROB-
ING QUESTIONS?
WHO HEARS MY HEART'S THOUGHTS?
       "BE STILL, MY PRECIOUS CHILD........"
   "DO YOU KNOW THAT I AM THE ANSWER TO YOUR
HEART'S QUEST?........"
"DO YOU KNOW WHO IS WHISPERING TO YOU DEEP IN
THE EMPTY CAVERNS OF YOUR HEART?........"

DID I HEAR SOMETHING DEEP WITHIN ME?
IS MY IMAGINATION RAISING GHOSTS OF HOPE TO MY
NEVER-ENDING THOUGHTS?
   ...."PRECIOUS LITTLE ONE, IT IS I SPEAKING........"
WHO SAID THAT?..........
HOW CAN I BE THINKING SUCH WORDS?............
........"BELOVED, I AM HE WHO HAS THE ANSWERS TO
YOUR HEART'S DESIRES........"

WHO ARE YOU, SPEAKING SO SOFTLY DEEP WITHIN
ME?
.........."IT IS I, YOUR FATHER........"
.........."IT IS I, YOUR DELIVERER........"
.........."IT IS I, YOUR COUNSELOR........"
       "COME!"

BY THE GRACE OF MY FATHER, NOW I KNOW HOW THE
STARS STAY IN POSITION IN THE HEAVENS!
BY THE LOVE OF MY KING, NOW I HAVE THE WARMTH
OF THE SON DEEPLY WITHIN ME, WARMING ALL THE
COLD EMPTY CAVERNS OF MY HEART!
BY MY FATHER, I SEE WHO SWIRLS THE SEAS IN
TURMOIL -
FOR MY FATHER'S ENEMY DESIRES THAT WHICH IS
NEVER TO BE - god!
BY MY SWEET COUNSELOR'S TEACHING, I AM NOW
FILLED WITH WONDROUS WISDOM!
FOR THOUGH I CANNOT SEE THE WIND, I FEEL THE
LOVING CARESSES ALL ABOUT ME!
ONCE I WAS SO BLIND BY MY SENSES, NOW I AM MY
FATHER'S CHILD,
THROUGH HIS EYES -
I SEE MY PURPOSE OF EXISTING -
THERE DEEP IN MY HEART, HE LIVES, KNOWING ALL
OF MY HEART'S DESIRES -
THEY ARE NOW FULFILLED!

(*Footnote)
Praise the Lord! Started and finished this on 12/16/94 while at
work!

JOURNEY OF LOVE

WHEN AT FIRST WE SET EYES UPON EACH OTHER -
A SEED OF LIFE I PLANTED DEEPLY INTO THEE -
HOW AT FIRST, MY BELOVED, DID YOU NOURISH MY
SEED!
YOU DRANK SO DEEPLY FROM THE WELL OF MY LIV-
ING WATER -
HOW YOU PARTOOK OF MY MANNA FROM THE
THRONE OF MY FATHER -
HOW BRIGHT YOU SHONE WITH MY HOLY SPIRIT'S
GLORY!
FROM A SEED, TO A YOUNG SAPLING, MY SEED OF
LOVE GREW DEEPLY WITHIN YOU -
EVEN AS A YOUNG TREE -
BUDS OF FRUIT SO PROMISING BLOSSOMED FORTH!
BUT, ALAS -
THE COOL WINDS OF CHANGE BLEW UPON THEE!
THE CLOUDS OF SORROW DEEPENED EVEN LIKE UNTO
NIGHTFALL -
TEARS RAN AS RIVERS OF DEATH SEEMED TO ENGULF
YOU -
YET, MY BELOVED -
DID YOU NOT KNOW THAT I DID NOT LEAVE YOU?

AS A MASTER BLACKSMITH TRIES AND MOLDS HIS
SWORD -
SO TOO, BELOVED, I BEGAN TO TRY AND MOLD YOU AS
I HAVE PREDESTINED YOU!

HAVE I NOT SPOKEN TO YOU IN THE WIND?
HAVE I NOT SPOKEN TO YOU IN THE RAIN?

HAVE I NOT SPOKEN TO YOU IN THE RAINBOW IN THE HEAVENS?
THE CRUEL DESOLATE WINDS AND STORMS OF WINTER HAVE PARCHED YOUR SOUL -
YET -
THERE IS SPRING AS A PROMISE OF RENEWED LIFE!
FOR EVERY NIGHT-FALL, THERE IS THE PROMISE OF DAWN!
SEE, MY BELOVED -
I AM THE BRIGHT MORNING STAR -
SHINING MY GLORY ROUND ABOUT YOU!
COME, PRECIOUS LITTLE ONE -
COME INTO THE SONSHINE!

COME INTO MY REST!
FOR I SHALL RENEW YOU, AND I SHALL RETURN TO YOU WHAT THE LOCUST HAS TAKEN FROM THEE!
SUSTAIN THYSELF DAILY UPON THE BREAD OF LIFE -
DRINK DEEPLY FROM THE WELL OF MY LIVING WATER -
RETURN TO THY FIRST LOVE -
BE MY MIGHTY TREE OF CEDAR -
BLOSSOM FORTH MY FRUITS OF LOVE, SO THAT THOSE WHOM I CHOOSE TO CROSS THY PATH -
SHALL KNOW THEIR KING, YOUR BELOVED BRIDEGROOM,
FOR I AM RETURNING SOON -
                    ARE YOU READY?

(* Footnote)
Praise the Lord! Started this at 3:30 P.M., finished this at 3.40 P.M.

29

GATEWAY INTO ETERNITY

IF ONLY I CAN GO BACK INTO MY YOUTH -
HOW I WOULD UNDO THE ERRORS OF MY FOOLISH
HEART!
IF ONLY I KNEW WHAT WAS TO BE TOMORROW -
HOW I CAN PLAN THE SECURITY OF MY LOVED ONES!
IF ONLY...................
SO MANY "IF ONLY".............
MOMENTS BECOME HOURS -
HOURS BECOME DAYS -
DAYS BECOME MONTHS -
MONTHS BECOME YEARS -
SO TIME PASSES -
NEVER TO BE GRASPED AGAIN!
YET -
IF ONLY................

BELOVED -
COME!
I AM THE ALPHA AND OMEGA -
I AM THE GATEWAY INTO ETERNITY -
FOLLOW ME -
AND I SHALL GUIDE THEE -
FOR I AM THE WAY -
IN THE DARKNESS OF YOUR DESPAIR -
LET MY LIGHT BE A LAMP UNTO THY FEET -
FOR I AM THE LIGHT OF THIS WORLD!
THOUGH YOU WERE IN DARKNESS YESTERDAY -
FEAR GRASPS YOUR HEART IN WORRY OF WHAT WILL
BE -
YET -

FEAR NOT!
MY WORDS ARE THE SAME AS THEY WERE YESTER-
DAY, TODAY, AND FOREVER!
THOUGH YOU KNEW ME NOT -
YET -
I KEPT THEE FROM ALL HARM!
DO NOT LET THE ENEMY ENTER INTO THY HOUSE -
FOR HE WILL KILL, ROB, AND DESTROY ALL THAT YOU
HOLD DEARLY!
SO DO NOT FRET, MY BELOVED -
DRAW NEAR TO ME -
ENTER INTO THE GATEWAY OF ETERNITY -
FOR I AM THE HEALER OF YOUR YESTERDAYS -
THY PROVIDER FOR THIS MOMENT -
THY HOPE FOR TOMORROW!

(*Footnote)
Praise the Lord! Started this on 12/22/94 at 8:00 A.M. and finished this at 8:15 A.M.

PROPHECY 7/27/92

ARISE! MY BELOVED CHILDREN!
ARISE, FROM THY SLUMBER!
IT IS TIME NOW TO GO FORTH!
IT IS TIME FOR JUBILATION!
THE TIME OF MOURNING IS PASSED -
NOW IT IS TIME TO GO FORTH IN THE LAND -
PROCLAIMING MY GLORY UNTO THE NATIONS!
YES!
MY BELOVED -
LET ME TRANSFORM YOU INTO MY PRESENCE AND
GLORY -
JUST LIKE THE BUTTERFLY NEEDED TO BE TRANS-
FORMED!
YES -
IT WAS A CATERPILLAR, GROUNDED TO THE EARTH -
YET -
IT KNEW WITHIN IT'S NATURE THAT IT WAS TIME -
IT WENT INTO IT'S COCOON, IT HAD TO DIE TO SELF!
YET -
SEE -
THE BEAUTIFUL BUTTERFLY EMERGE FROM THAT
COCOON OF DEATH!
SEE -
HOW IT SOARS IN THE HEAVENLIES!

NOW, BELOVED, IT IS TIME TO COME OUT OF THIS
WORLD -
THIS COCOON OF DEATH!
NOW, BELOVED, IT IS TIME TO BECOME GLORIOUS IN
ME!

COME, BELOVED, LET US SOAR IN THE HEAVENLIES IN
GREAT EXALTATION!
FOR ALL TO SEE -
I AM MIGHTY IN YOU!
SO, COME, LET US TAKE FLIGHT!
LET ME HEAL YOU,
LET ME TEACH YOU,
THE FATHER'S WISDOM -
FOR HIS WISDOM IS LIFE UNTO YOU, MY BELOVED!

THE FATHER'S LOVE

PROPHECY OF 11/29/92

COME! MY BELOVED CHILDREN!
COME UNTO ME!
LOOK ONLY TO ME FOR ALL YOUR NEEDS -
FOR AS YOUR FATHER, I WOULD LAVISH UPON YOU
ALL GOOD BLESSINGS -
NO. MY BELOVED CHILDREN -
I WILL NOT CAUSE YOU TO CARRY A BURDEN THAT
YOU CANNOT CARRY -
THAT IS WHY I'VE GIVEN YOU MY ULTIMATE GIFT OF
LOVE -
MY ONLY BEGOTTEN SON - JESUS OF NAZARETH!

YES! BELOVED -
COME!
COME TO CALVARY -
COME TO THE FOUNDATION OF YOUR SALVATION!
COME AND REFRESH YOURSELVES!
DO NOT LOOK TO THIS WORLD FOR YOUR SALVATION -
BUT LOOK TO THE CROSS OF LIFE!
YES!
THE CROSS OF YOUR LIFE -
BOUGHT WITH THE PRECIOUS BLOOD OF JESUS OF
NAZARETH!
HEAR MY BELOVED, ALL THE ANGELIC HOSTS ARE
WALKING BESIDE YOU -
BATTLING THE RAVENOUS ONSLAUGHT OF OUR
ENEMY!
BUT FEAR NOT!
I WILL NEVER FORSAKE YOU!
I WILL BE WITH YOU ALWAYS!

LET MY LOVE COVER AND HEAL YOU!
LET US WALK IN JOYOUS VICTORY -
FOR MY LOVE IS YOUR HEALING IN THESE TIMES OF
DISTRESS!

(*Footnote)
Praise the Lord! Truly the Lord is good!

PROPHECY 9/7/93 AT 3:30 P.M.

OH! MY LITTLE ONES -
YES -
I CALL YOU SUCH!
BE NOT OFFENDED -
FOR IT IS IN PURE LOVE I CALL YOU -
"LITTLE ONE"!
JUST AS AN EARTHLY FATHER LOVINGLY CALLS HIS
CHILDREN -
"LITTLE ONES"!
BE NOT FRETFUL -
BE NOT GRIEVED -
THOUGH IT BE NIGHT -
YET -
SEE THE DIAMONDS OF HOPE IN THE BLACKNESS!

BE NOT DISMAYED THAT THE ENEMY SEEMS TO TEAR
AT YOU -
HAVE I NOT GIVEN YOU THE FULL ARMOR OF FAITH?
HAVE I NOT SPOKEN THAT "NO WEAPON FORMED
AGAINST SHALL NOT PREVAIL"!
YES! BELOVED!
MY WORDS ARE FULL OF POWER -
THEY DO NOT GO FORTH EMPTY -
BUT THEY RETURN TO ME FULFILLED!
FOR YOUR FAITH, BRINGS MY HEART TO BE DRAWN TO
YOUR SUPPLICATIONS -
AND I HAVE MADE A COVENANT WITH YOUR FORE-
FATHERS -
"I SHALL BLESS YOUR SEED AND THEIR SEEDS -
"I SHALL MULTIPLY THEM -

38

"THEY SHALL BE MY CROWN OF GLORY"!

SO FEAR NOT!
FOR NIGHT IS VANQUISHED AT THE FIRST BRIGHT
MORNING LIGHT -
I AM YOUR BRIGHT MORNING STAR!
SO HOLD FAST TO MY DIAMONDS OF HOPE THAT BURN
BRILLIANTLY IN THE NIGHT CANVAS OF DESPAIR!

A FATHER'S LOVE!

WHEN I WAS BUT A SMALL YOUNG CHILD,
HOW I USED TO SIT BY THE WINDOW WAITING FOR MY
DADDY TO COME HOME!
TALL AS A TREE, HAIR THE COLOR OF AUTUMN
LEAVES,
WITH TIRED EYES SO GREEN AND BRIGHT -
WITH A SMILE THAT MADE ME FEEL SO WARM AND
TINGLY -
I WOULD RUN TO HIS OUTSTRETCHED ARMS,
AND HE WOULD HUG ME, OH! SO TIGHTLY!
HOW I LOVED MY DADDY!

ONE DAY, I WAS NAUGHTY -
I GRABBED MY DOLL AWAY FROM MY SISTER,
I HIT HER BECAUSE I WAS MAD AT HER FOR ALWAYS
TAKING MY TOYS,
I CALLED HER NAMES AND LIKE A CRY BABY,
SHE RAN AND TATTLETAILED TO OUR DAD!
TALL AS A TREE,
HAIR THE COLOR OF FLAME,
WITH BLAZING GREEN EYES OF ANGER,
HE MARCHED TOWARDS ME,
IT SEEMED THE WHOLE HOUSE SHOOK WITH EACH OF
HIS STEPS!
I SUDDENLY FELT SO AFRAID!
I RAN TO MY ROOM, AND HID IN THE CLOSET!
BUT DADDY FOUND ME ANYWAY!
HE OPENED THE DOOR SO HARD, I THOUGHT THE
DOOR WAS BROKE -

HE GRABBED ME BY MY HAND AND PULLED ME OUT
OF THE CLOSET -
I SCREAMED!
"DADDY!"
"NO!"
"I'LL BE GOOD!"
"DADDY!"
"NO!"
"I'M SORRY!"
HE LAID ME ACROSS HIS LAP -
AND WITH A HARD LEATHER STRAP -
HE STRIKED AT MY TINY BOTTOM TILL IT REALLY
HURT SO BAD!
I SCREAMED AND CRIED FOR HIM TO STOP -
FINALLY -
WHEN I THOUGHT HE WAS GOING TO KILL ME -
HE STOPPED!
LATER THAT EVENING -
QUIETLY HE CAME TO MY DOOR,
HE KNOCKED SO SOFTLY, I BARELY HEARD -
QUIETLY, HE BEGGED TO LET HIM IN,
I WAS STILL CRYING -
I WAS STILL HURTING.
I WAS SO AFRAID OF HIM -
I THOUGHT HE WOULD HIT ME AGAIN!
BUT HE WAS MY DADDY, MY ONE AND ONLY DADDY,
AND I LOVED HIM SO VERY MUCH!
SO, I OPENED THE DOOR -
THERE HE STOOD -
TALL AS A GIANT -
HAIR THE COLOR OF WINE -
SAD, TEARFUL EYES OF LIQUID GREEN -
A LITTLE SMILE -
HIS ARMS OUTSTRETCHED -
I HESITATED TO RUN INTO HIS WARM EMBRACE -
HE SAW MY FEAR -

HE FELT MY PAIN -
SOFTLY HE SAID:
"MY PRECIOUS LITTLE ONE -
"I'M SORRY I HAD TO PUNISH YOU, BUT IT'S BECAUSE I
LOVE YOU SO VERY MUCH THAT I HAD TO HURT YOU,
SO THAT YOU WILL LEARN THAT
"YOU CANNOT BE SELFISH WITH YOUR THINGS.
"YOU'VE GOT TO SHARE WITH YOUR SISTER BECAUSE
I LOVE HER TOO!
"WHATEVER I GIVE, IT'S NOT JUST FOR YOU, IT'S FOR
HER TOO.
"AND SHE HAS TO BE THE SAME WAY TOO.
"I HAD TO GIVE YOU PAIN, AS YOU GAVE PAIN TO YOUR
SISTER,
"BECAUSE AFTER ALL, SHE HAS THE SAME BLOOD AS
YOU AND ME.
"WE ARE A FAMILY AND WE SHOULD MAKE EACH
OTHER HAPPY AND LOVE ONE ANOTHER, JUST LIKE I
DO.
"SO, MY PRECIOUS LITTLE ONE, COME HERE, LET ME
MAKE YOU FEEL BETTER"!
AT THAT -
I RAN INTO HIS ARMS AND I CRIED!
BUT THIS TIME, THE PAIN DIDN'T HURT ANYMORE!
THEN HE TOOK MY HAND AND WE WENT TO MY SIS-
TER'S ROOM,
SHE HAD HER BACK TO US, SHE WOULDN'T LET ME
TALK TO HER.
THEN DADDY STRETCHED HIS BIG LONG ARMS AND
FOLDED US IN HIS EMBRACE TOGETHER!
WE ALL LAUGHED, TICKLED EACH OTHER AND
HUGGED -
WE SAID: "I'M SORRY TO EACH OTHER, THEN WE
KISSED EACH OTHER, AND WE SAID: "I LOVE YOU"!

TODAY, LOOKING BACK -

MY HEART ACHES -
FOR I SO MISS MY DAD!
AND I PRAY THAT WHEREVER HE IS -
THAT HE'S O.K. AND HAPPY.
TODAY, AS MY SISTER AND I JOIN HANDS IN PRAYER -
WE THANK GOD FOR THE JOY AND BLESSINGS WE'VE
SHARED IN EACH OTHER'S LIVES -
AND WITH OUR CHILDREN GATHERED AROUND US IN
AN UNBROKEN CIRCLE OF LOVE -
WE READ FROM THE HOLY WORD OF GOD, FOR HE IS
OUR HEAVENLY FATHER.

OUR ONE AND ONLY FATHER -
MADE POSSIBLE BY THE MIRACLE OF CALVARY -
THERE HE CONFIRMS OUR INHERITANCE OF EVER-
LASTING LIFE AS HIS CHILDREN AND WE CONFIRM HIS
LOVE BY OUR SHARING, CARING, LOVING,
HELPING, PRAYING AND WORSHIPPING HIM TOGETH-
ER AS ONE BIG FAMILY IN HIM MADE POSSIBLE BY HIS
GREAT GIFT OF LOVE -
JESUS OF NAZARETH!
FOR IF WE ARE NOT HIS CHILDREN -
THEN WE ARE ILLEGITIMATE, AND THEN WE WOULD
BE CHILDREN OF DARKNESS AND OUR FATHER
WOULD BE THE PRINCE OF THIS WORLD AND WE
WOULD SUFFER HIS HATE BY ACTS OF MURDER, SLAN-
DER, IMMORALITY,
FORNICATION AND EVERY DARK DEATHLY DEED TO
ONE ANOTHER!
SO, HERE I AM TODAY -
SO VERY GRATEFUL FOR THE PAINFUL LESSON OF
LOVE -
MY GENTLE, LOVING DADDY HAD TO AFFLICT ME SO
VERY, VERY LONG -
AGO!
BECAUSE HE REALLY LOVED ME AND ONLY WANTED

ME TO BE JUST LIKE HIM!
SO, NOW AS I SIT HERE READING THE LORD'S WORDS -
I CAN SEE THAT MY HEAVENLY FATHER EVERY NOW
AND THEN NEEDS TO CHASTISE ME -
AND THRU TEARS OF UNDERSTANDING I THANK MY
HEAVENLY FATHER EVEN IN THE TRYING, PAINFUL
TIMES, BECAUSE I HAVE HIS PROMISE IN MY HEART -
"NEVER WILL I LEAVE YOU OR FORSAKE YOU"!

(*Footnote)
Praise the Lord! 1/1/90

A FATHER'S LOVE CALL!

OH! MY BELOVED CHILDREN -
YES, I CALL THEE MY CHILD -
FOR I HAVE CREATED YOU FOR MY PLEASURE -
IN MY IMAGE I HAVE CREATED YOU -
IN LOVE I FASHIONED THEE -
MY BREATH -
MY GIFT OF LIFE I BREATHED INTO YOUR SOUL -
AND YOU WERE CREATED IN MY IMAGE!
IN LONGING TO FELLOWSHIP -
I'VE CREATED YOU -
ALL THE HEAVENLY HOSTS MARVEL OF YOUR
CREATION -
FOR I HAVE MADE YOU A LITTLE HIGHER THAN THE
ANGELIC HOSTS -
YET -
THOUGH YOU BE LOWER THAN THEY -
YET -
IN MY SON'S HOLY NAME -
I'VE GIVEN YOU DOMINION OVER ALL OF MY CREATION!

OH! MY BELOVED CHILD -
DO YOU FEEL MY TEARDROPS IN THE RAIN?
DO YOU HEAR MY VOICE IN THE ROLLING THUNDER?
DO YOU SEE THE FIERY FLASH OF MY ANGER -
WHEN YOU CHOOSE TO WORSHIP DEAD FALSE GODS!
DO YOU FEEL MY GENTLE CARESSES OF FORGIVENESS
IN THE BREEZE?
ARE YOU FIRMLY ANCHORED IN MY BELOVED SON?

WHEN THE FURIOUS WINDS OF HATE TEAR AT YOU -
ARE YOU UPROOTED?
ARE YOU EASILY PERSUADED BY THE CURRENTS OF
THIS WORLD?
DO YOU SMELL THE FRAGRANT PUNGENT AROMA OF
MY ANOINTED PRESENCE?
OR DO YOU SMELL THE STENCH OF MY ADVERSARY'S
PRESENCE?
IN YOUR INFREQUENT PRAYERS -
DO YOU BESEECH ME TO VINDICATE MY WRATH UPON
YOUR ENEMIES -
OR DO YOU EARNESTLY SEEK MY MERCY AND BLESS-
INGS UPON YOUR ENEMIES?
HAVE I NOT SPOKEN -
BLESS YOUR ENEMIES -
LOVE YOU ENEMY -
FEED AND CLOTHE YOUR ENEMY -
FOR IN DOING SO -
THE WORLD WOULD SEE MY GLORY THROUGH YOU!
HAVE YOU NOT SEEN HOW GREAT MY LOVE IS FOR
YOU -
WHEN MY ONLY BEGOTTEN SON WAS RAISED UPON A
DEADENED TREE -
DID HE BESEECH ME TO VANQUISH HIS ENEMIES -
OR HAVE YOU HEARD MY SON CRY OUT -
"FATHER! FATHER! FORGIVE THEM! FOR THEY KNOW
NOT WHAT THEY HAVE DONE!"

OH! MY BELOVED CHILD -
YES -
THOUGH YOU BE GRAY AND FRAIL -
YET -
YOU ARE MY BELOVED CHILD!
THOUGH YOU BE IN SWADDLING CLOTH -
YET -
YOU ARE MY BELOVED CHILD!

THOUGH YOU BE A REBELLIOUS CHILD -
YET -
YOU ARE MY BELOVED CHILD!
THOUGH YOU BE A YOUNG MAN -
SEARCHING FOR TRUTH -
MISLEAD ON THE WIDE ROAD OF DEATH -
BY YOUR FRIENDS -
YET -
YOU ARE MY BELOVED CHILD!

BE NOT OFFENDED THAT I ADDRESS YOU AS MY CHILD -
BE HONORED THAT I HAVE CALLED YOU -
I HAVE YOUR NAME CARVED IN THE PALMS OF MY
HANDS -
NONE -
CAN TAKE THEE AWAY FROM ME!

YES, MY BELOVED -
THOUGH THERE BE TEMPESTS AND DELUGE -
AND FIERY TRAILS -
YET -
MY HAND IS UPON THEE!
DO NOT FEAR -
FOR AS A LOVING FATHER CHASTISES HIS CHILDREN -
SO I, TOO, WILL CHASTISE THEE!
PRAISE ME, IN THOSE TROUBLED WEARY TIMES!
PRAISE ME, FOR USING MY ADVERSARY'S HATRED TO
BRING UPON YOU THE TRIALS AND PERSECUTIONS -
FOR I AM FASHIONING A MIGHTY WEAPON TO
DESTROY OUR ENEMY!

YES, MY BELOVED,
HE IS MY ADVERSARY FROM THE FOUNDATION OF
TIME -
YET -
HE IS ALSO YOUR ENEMY -

SO GREAT HAS HIS HEART GROWN IN REBELLION
AGAINST ME -
A god HE DESIRES TO BE -
WORSHIP, PRAISE AND HONOR HE DEMANDS!
A CRUEL TASKMASTER IS HE TO THOSE WHOM HE
ENSLAVES!

YES, BELOVED -
IN THE DARKNESS OF YOUR DESPAIR -
IN THE PIT OF DEATH -
BY MY SON'S SHED INNOCENT BLOOD
I SNATCHED THEE OUT OF THE ENEMIES CAMP!

YES, BELOVED -
AS MOSES LED MY PEOPLE OUT OF EGYPT -
SO, MY BELOVED SON, JESUS, DELIVERED YOU FROM
EVERLASTING DAMNATION!
WHEN YOU RECEIVED MY SON -
WHEN YOU CHOSE TO HAVE MY SON -
RULE AND REIGN IN YOUR HEART -
WHEN YOU WILLINGLY SAW THE DARKNESS WITHIN
YOU BY THE LIGHT OF MY WORD -
AND YOU ASKED FOR MY FORGIVENESS -
AND YOU CLEANSED YOURSELF BY THE SHED BLOOD
OF ATONEMENT OF MY SON AS YOUR SACRIFICIAL
LAMB -
IT IS THEN, MY BELOVED,
YOU ARE MY CHILD!
IT IS THEN, MY BELOVED,
YOU HAVE ENTERED INTO MY KINGDOM!
IT IS IN THAT ATONING MOMENT -
YOU BECOME CO-HEIR WITH MY SON -
IN THAT MOMENT -

COMMAND YE ME -
FOR I SHALL FULFILL MY WORD!
MY WORDS DO NOT GO FORTH VOID -
THEY RETURN FULL OF POWER -
THE POWER OF YOUR FAITH!

YES, MY BELOVED -
THEREIN LIES THE SECRET -
WHICH IN MY GRACE, I ILLUMINATE THIS IN YOUR
SPIRIT BY THE POWER OF MY HOLY SPIRIT!
SEEK ME EARNESTLY, MY BELOVED!
PRAISE ME WITH THY WHOLE HEART -
FOR IN PRAISE LIES YOUR STRENGTH AND YOUR
VICTORY!

HEAR ME, O! MY HOLY MOUNTAIN OF ZION!
GREAT WILL BE THY REWARD -
STAND FIRM UPON THE CORNERSTONE OF EMMANUEL!
FOR HE IS YOUR DELIVERER -
    HE IS YOUR PROTECTOR -
    HE IS THE LION OF THE TRIBE OF JUDAH!
DO YOU HEAR HIS MIGHTY ROAR IN THE LAND OF
GIANTS?
THE ENEMY TREMBLES -
FOR HE KNOWS HIS TIME IS SHORT!
FOR A TIME, BELOVED -
IN THE MIDNIGHT DARKNESS OF NIGHT -
HE WILL SEEK TO DESTROY YOU -
HE WILL SEEK TO TEAR YOU APART -
HE WILL SEEK TO LURE YOU UPON THE PATH OF
DESTRUCTION!
BUT -
FEAR NOT!
THE GATES OF HELL SHALL NOT PREVAIL AGAINST
THEE!

FOR I HAVE FASHIONED YOU SINCE TIME BEGAN TO BE
MY SON'S BRIDE!

AWAKE, MY BELOVED!
ARISE, MY BELOVED!
NOW IS THE MOMENT OF GREAT LABOR -
FOR THE FIELDS ARE WHITE -
GREAT IS THE HARVEST!
SOON, BELOVED, NIGHT WILL BE UPON YOU -
ALL LABOR WILL CEASE -
DO YOU HEAR THE WATCHMAN SOUNDING HIS TRUM-
PET?
THE ENEMY IS AT THE GATE OF YOUR SOUL -
BUT FEAR NOT!
FOR I AM WITH YOU ALWAYS!
TOGETHER WE SHALL WALK THROUGH THE FIERY
FURNACE OF OUR ENEMY'S HATRED -
YOU WILL NOT BE SCORCHED -
FOR IN THE FIRE, ALL SHALL WITNESS MY GLORY
WITHIN YOU!

OH! MY BELOVED -
ARE YOU STILL REJECTING MY LOVE?
WHY DO YOU RUN AFTER OTHER "gods"?
DO THEY SPEAK TO YOU?
DO THEY HEAR YOUR PRAYERS?
DO THEY SHOWER YOU WITH GOOD GIFTS?
BE NOT FOOLISH, MY BELOVED!
I AM THE LORD THY GOD!
I AM A JEALOUS GOD -
I WILL NOT HAVE ANY OTHER "gods" BEFORE ME!

OH! MY BELOVED -
DO NOT DRINK FROM THE HARLOT'S CUP!
FOR IF YOU CHOOSE TO DO SO -

THEN YOU SHALL DRINK FROM THE WINEPRESS OF
MY WRATH!
OH! MY BELOVED -
DO NOT FEAST WITH MY ENEMIES -
FOR IF YOU CHOOSE TO DO SO -
THEN YOU SHALL FEAST UPON THE CARRION OF MY
ANGER AGAINST THEE!
MY CHILDREN IN EGYPT -
DELIVERED FROM THE PHAROAH'S TYRANNY -
BROUGHT INTO THE WILDERNESS -
SO THEY MAY BE REFINED AS PURE GOLD -
THEY CRIED OUT TO ME FOR THE MEAT OF THEIR
LUSTY DESIRES!
AND SO, I GRANTED THEIR PRAYERS -
I FED THEM DAILY MANNA FROM THE HEAVENLY
PLACES -
THE BREAD OF MY ANGELS -
YET -
THEY REFUSED -
FOR IT WAS NOT SUITABLE FOR THEIR NATURAL
APPETITE!
SEE, MY BELOVED -
AS A LOVING FATHER -
I KNOW WHAT GOOD GIFTS TO GIVE YOU -
TRUST ME, BELOVED -
I HAVE GOOD PLANS FOR YOUR TOMORROWS -
NOT EVIL!
BE NOT FOOLISH AS THE RICH YOUNG MAN, WHO
QUESTIONED MY SON -
"MASTER -
"HOW MAY I ENTER YOUR KINGDOM?"
JESUS REPLIED:
"SELL ALL OF YOUR GOODS -
"GIVE THEM TO THE NEEDY AND THE POOR -
"THEN YOU SHALL ENTER MY KINGDOM!"
HOW IT SADDENED THE YOUNG MAN TO HEAR THOSE

HARSH WORDS!
HE FREELY CHOSE TO REJECT SUCH AN OFFER -
FOR THE TREASURES OF HIS HEART WAS CHAINED TO
HIS RICHES!
REMEMBER MY WORDS, MY BELOVED -
"BLESSED BE THE POOR IN SPIRIT -
"FOR THEY SHALL INHERIT MY KINGDOM!"
"A MAN'S HEART IS WHERE HIS TREASURE LIES!"

DO YOU NOT SEE, MY BELOVED -
MY WORDS ARE TRUTH -
MY WORDS ARE LIFE INTO THEE -
MY WORDS ARE A LAMP UNTO THY FEET -
FOR MY WORDS WILL GUIDE YOU TO EVERLASTING
LIFE!
DO YOU NOT UNDERSTAND, MY BELOVED -
MY WORDS ARE EVERLASTING -
MY WORDS ARE CONDITIONAL -
NOT TO BE INTERPRETED BY YOUR PERCEPTION OF
UNDERSTANDING -
FOR MAN'S THOUGHTS ARE NOT MY THOUGHTS -
AND YOUR THOUGHTS ARE NOT MINE!
THE NATURE OF SIN HAS CHANGED YOU -
YOU NO LONGER ARE OF MY IMAGE -
BUT OF MY ENEMY -
AND THE DESIRES OF YOUR HEART ARE CARNAL!

HEAR ME, MY BELOVED -
SEEK WISDOM -
AS SOLOMON DESIRED A GOOD GIFT -
I POURED OUT MY HOLY SPIRIT UPON HIM -
HIS COLD STONY HEART WAS BROKEN BY THE
MIGHTY SCEPTER OF MY JUDGEMENT -
OH! MY BELOVED -
TIS IS THE TREASURE OF MY HEART -
THAT YOU AND I CAN FELLOWSHIP -

THAT YOU AND I CAN BE ONE!
AS MY SON PRAYED -
"FATHER, I PRAY FOR THESE WHOM YOU'VE CHOSEN,
"THAT THEY WILL BE ONE, AS WE ARE ONE!"

MY BELOVED BRIDE -
I HAVE CALLED THEE FROM THE VERY DEPTHS OF THE
SEA -
COME, AWAY WITH ME, MY BELOVED!
ARISE AND SHINE GLORIOUSLY IN THIS DYING WORLD -
LET ALL SEE THE GLORY OF THEIR HOPE -
HIGH UPON A HILL CALLED GOLGOTHA -
OUTSIDE THE CITY GATES -
UPON A CURSED TREE BRANCH -
EYES SERENELY GAZING INTO THE HEAVENS -
WITH ARMS STRETCHED OUT -
FROM TIME BEGINNING -

```
                        E
                        M
                        M
            ALPHA       A    OMEGA
                        N
                        U
                        E
                        L
```

TO TIME ENDING -
EVEN INTO EVERLASTING -
EMBRACING YOU, BELOVED -
WITH A LOVE SO GREAT -
THAT I'VE GIVEN YOU MY ONLY BEGOTTEN SON -
"EMMANUEL -"
"THE LORD IS WITH THEE"!

SO REJOICE, MY BELOVED!
PRAISE ME -
YES, PRAISE IS THE KEY TO VICTORY!
PRAISE IS THE TRUMPET SOUND OF DEATH TO OUR
ENEMIES!
PRAISE WILL BREAK DOWN THE WALLS OF OPPRES-
SION -
JUST AS PRAISE BROUGHT THE WALLS OF JERICHO
TUMBLING DOWN!
PRAISE ME, BELOVED -
NOT THAT I NEED YOUR PRAISES -
BUT I WILL BE DRAWN TO YOU -
AS PRAISE WILL DRAW YOU TO ME -
FOR IT IS IN HEART PRAISE -
THAT YOUR SPIRIT ARISES -
IN THAT MOMENT OF HIGHEST PRAISE, WE ARE ONE!
IN PRAISE, MY GLORY WILL ENFOLD YOU -
IN PRAISE, THE ENEMY WILL FLEE -
IN PRAISE, MY HEALING BALM WILL FLOW UPON THEE -
LIKE AARON'S ANOINTING FLOWING FROM THE
CROWN OF HIS HEAD -
DOWN HIS LONG FLOWING BEARD -
DOWN TO HIS FEET!

YES, MY BELOVED BRIDE -
SING PRAISES OF JOY!
DANCE IN ABANDONMENT AS DAVID DANCED TO HIS
LORD!
IN DOING SO, MY LIFE WILL FLOW DEEPLY WITHIN
YOU -
ALL WILL SEE MY GLORY SHINE THROUGH YOU -
THE LOST -
THE WOUNDED -
THE SEEKING -
SHALL LOOK UPON THEE -
AND THEY WILL KNOW -

I AM THE LORD AND GOD OF ISRAEL -
I AM THE LORD AND GOD OF MT. ZION -
I AM ETERNAL LIFE!

(*Footnote) Praise and glory and honor to my God, forever and ever, Amen! Started this 4/11/94 at 9:15 A.M.; finished this intermittently through the hours of work, the Lord spoke His heart to His child, ended at 2:30 P.M. now His child - His Son's Bride shouts a war cry of victory -

JESUS OF NAZARETH IS ALIVE!

DESIRE!

LORD!
HEAR ME! I MAY BE SMALL IN YOUR EYES, BUT -
LORD!
HEAR ME!
GRANT THAT MY PRAYERS BE ANSWERED!
LORD!
I NEED A BIGGER HOUSE!
IT'S NOT FAIR THAT YOU GAVE MY NEIGHBOR A BET-
TER PLACE TO LIVE THAN US LORD!
I NEED A NEW CAR, IT'S NOT FAIR THAT YOU GAVE MY
NEIGHBOR A BRIGHT NEW SHINING CAR AND I HAVE
TO USE THIS OLD RIGGETY JUNK!
LORD!
I NEED A BETTER PAYING JOB, I CAN'T LIVE LIKE MY
NEXT DOOR NEIGHBOR WITHOUT BECOMING
LAUGHED AT AND ASHAMED!

CHILD!
I HEAR YOUR SELFISH NEEDS AND DESIRES,
BUT -
DO YOU HEAR ME?
DO YOU HEAR ME SAY:
"CHILD"!
"HEAR ME "!
"I HAVE NO PLACE OF SHELTER"!
"THIS OLD CARDBOARD BOX WILL NOT KEEP ME
WARM, IT WILL NOT KEEP ME DRY WHEN IT RAINS,
AND SHOULD A STORM COME - I WILL LOSE EVEN THIS
SMALL HAVEN"!
"CHILD"!

"HEAR ME"!

"I AM WALKING THE STREETS SEEKING A PLACE OF WARMTH AND LOVE,

CARS GO BY, PEOPLE WALK BY ME,

BUT -

"THEY DO NOT SEE ME, THEY DO NOT HEAR ME"!

"CHILD"!

"DO YOU SEE ME"?

"I AM THAT DIRTY RAGGEDY STREET BUM BEGGING FOR A DIME SO THAT I MIGHT HAVE SOMETHING TO DRINK, SOMETHING TO EAT, SOMEWHERE TO REST AT DAY'S END"!

"CHILD"!

"I HAVE DESIRES ALSO"!

"I DESIRE THAT YOU LOVE ME"!

"I DESIRE THAT YOU HAVE COMPASSION -

"I DESIRE THAT YOU WILL INVITE ME INTO YOUR HOME"!

"I DESIRE THAT YOU FEED ME, CARE FOR ME, THERE IS YOUR REWARD"!

"FOR THERE YOU WILL FIND A KINGDOM OF SUCH SPLENDOR -

     THERE YOU WILL NEVER NEED A SHELTER -

     THERE YOU WILL NEVER NEED FOOD OR DRINK!

     THERE YOU WILL NEVER SUFFER OR DIE"!

HOUSE OF STONE!

OH! COME AND SEE MY NEW HOUSE!
SEE HOW FINE THE BRICKLAYERS HAVE LAID THEIR
STONE TO PERFECTION!
COME AND SEE MY SPACIOUS ROOMS -
SO FILLED WITH DELIGHTFUL TREASURES I HAVE
FOUND IN THE MARKET-PLACE!
COME AND SHARE MY JOY!

"IN THREE DAYS, I SHALL REBUILD THIS TEMPLE!"
WHO SPOKE SUCH WORDS AS FOOLISH AS THESE?
FOR IT HAS TAKEN FORTY YEARS FOR THIS TEMPLE TO
BE BUILT!
IS THIS MAN A SORCERER - OR A MAD MAN?
SEE, HOW THE PEOPLE GAZE AT THE INTRICATE
DETAILS THE STONECUTTER WROUGHT WITH HIS
SKILL!
NOW, WHO SPEAKS -
"IN THREE DAYS I SHALL REBUILD THIS TEMPLE?"

QUIETLY, A SMALL BAND GATHER IN A ROOM WHERE
THERE IS NO INTRICATE BEAUTY CUT INTO THE
WALLS,
NO CRAFTSMENSHIP CAN LAY CLAIM TO THE WORK
THAT IS BEING DONE NOW!
THESE FEW VOICES RISE TO THE HEAVENS -
AND THEIR SONG IS JOINED BY THE HEAVENLY HOSTS!
HANDS RAISED ON HIGH -
EYES IN POOLS OF JOY -
HEARTS BLOOMING WITH THE SWEET FRAGRANCES
OF PRAYERS UNSPOKEN -

NO ROOM -
NO TEMPLE OF STONE -
CAN CONTAIN THE AWESOME PRESENCE OF OUR
LORD!
FOR INDEED HE HAS REBUILT THIS TEMPLE -
IN THE THREE DAYS HE WAS IN THE BELLY OF DEATH -
HE DESTROYED THE STINGER'S DEATH BLOWS -
AND HE RAISED ME UP -
SO I MUST PROCLAIM -
COME!
WELCOME TO MY LORD'S HOUSE OF LOVE!
HERE IN HIS BOSOM, YOU FIND PEACE AND SOLITUDE
FROM THE CLAMORING OF THIS WORLD!
COME AND SIT BY HIS FEET -
FOR HE SHALL FILL THE DRY PLACES WITH THE WELL-
SPRING OF LIVING WATERS!
DRINK AND EAT DEEPLY FROM THE MASTER'S SUPPER
TABLE!
WE HIS SERVANTS WILL CLEANSE AND REFRESH THEE!
FOR THY DAYS OF WANDERING IN THE WILDERNESS
ARE OVER!
FOR HE HAS CALLED YOU IN THE WINDS OF CHANGE
THAT BLOW IN THIS LAND OF FAMINE -
NOW, AS HE HAS PROMISED -
"MY FATHER HAS A ROOM PREPARED FOR YOU" -
FOR HE HAS A MANSION FILLED WITH MANY ROOMS -
FOR IN THIS HOUSE -
ABBA FATHER IS OUR SOVEREIGN LORD -
HIS SON - JESUS IS OUR KING AND LORD -
HIS HOLY SPIRIT IS OUR COMFORTER AND OUR COUN-
SELOR -
WHAT HAND CAN CLAIM THE MIGHTY WORK THAT
HAS BEGUN BEFORE THE FOUNDATION OF TIME?
FOR MEN BUILD HOUSES OF STONE THAT OTHER MEN
CAN DESTROY -
BUT CANNOT BE REBUILT -

FOR THE STONECUTTER IS A SIGNATURE OF HIS CRAFT
THAT NO ONE ELSE CAN FORGE -
SO TOO -
A YOUNG MAN, IN A BUSTLING CITY FILLED WITH
TEMPLES OF STONE CRIED OUT: -
"I CAN REBUILD THIS TEMPLE IN THREE DAYS!"
DID ANYONE SEE WHAT TEMPLE HE WAS POINTING AT?
DID ANYONE SEE WHAT TEMPLE HE WAS REFERRING
TO?
FOR HE REMARKED WHAT HIS FATHER HAS PRO-
CLAIMED FROM ABRAHAM'S
                    SEED -
"OUT OF THY SEED - I SHALL RAISE UP A PEOPLE, THEY
SHALL BE MY PEOPLE,
AND I WILL BE THEIR GOD!"
SO COME INTO MY HOME -
THOUGH IT MIGHT BE MEAGER IN THE EYES OF MY
BRETHERN -
YET -
THE PRESENCE OF MY LORD FILLS THIS PLACE -
THOUGH I GIVE YOU FOOD FOR YOUR BODY -
HE WILL SATISFY YOUR HEART'S DESIRE!
FOR I AM HIS SERVANT - COME IN - BE REFRESHED AND
RENEWED IN MY FATHER'S HOUSE!

(*FOOTNOTE)
Praise the Lord! Started this on 5/7/96 at 3:30 A.M., finished this
at 4:10 A.M. By His Holy Spirit my heart rejoices at His goodness and mercy towards His servant!

HIS BANNER
OVER ME IS LOVE!

A GIFT OF LOVE

IN THE PAGES OF MAN'S HISTORY -
IN A TIME WHEN DARKNESS REIGNED -
IN A TIME OF CRUEL MASTERS, AND OPPRESSED
SLAVES -
IN A TIME OF HOPELESSNESS AND DESPAIR -
A WONDROUS STAR APPEARED IN THE HEAVENS!
SHEPHERDS GAZED IN WONDER -
KINGS GAZED AND FOLLOWED IT'S SILVERY PATH -
THE CRUEL MASTERS MOANED FOR THEY KNEW IT
WOULD BRING LIGHT INTO THEIR DARK KINGDOM!
THE DESTITUTE SLAVES GAZED UPON THIS WON-
DROUS STAR -
THEIR HEARTS REJOICED!
FOR THEY KNEW THAT THE PROPHECIES OF OLD
PROPHETS BROUGHT A MESSAGE OF HOPE -
THEIR MESSIAH WAS COMING TO DELIVER THEM!

IN A SLEEPY LITTLE TOWN CALLED BETHLEHEM -
IN AN INNKEEPER'S STABLE -
A BABY'S CRY BROKE THE MIDNIGHT STILLNESS!
UPON THE THATCHED ROOF, STREAMS OF SILVERY
BEAMS BATHED THE NEWBORN BABE -
GLORIOUS ANGELS SANG LULLABIES TO THEIR KING -
GLORIOUS ANGELS SANG TIDINGS OF JOY TO THE
SHEPHERDS WATCHING OVER THEIR SHEEP!
ALL WHO HEARD THIS HEAVENLY CHOIR, GATHERED
AT THE MANGER -
IN ADORATION THEY KNELT BEFORE A BABE WRAPPED
IN SWADDLING CLOTH!
THEIR HEARTS AFLAME WITH HOPE -

HERE BEFORE THEM WAS THEIR GIFT OF LOVE!
SENT BY THEIR HEAVENLY FATHER HIGH ABOVE IN
THE HEAVENS -
AND THE NIGHT GROANED AND GNASHED IT'S TEETH!

IN THE HEART OF THE WILDERNESS A MAGNIFICENT
CITY SHONE AS A JEWEL -
ONE DAY A CHILD WENT IN A TEMPLE -
HOW HE AMAZED THE ELDERLY SCHOLARS!
A CHILD OF WISDOM, THEY WHISPERED -
COULD HE BE OUR LONG AWAITED MESSIAH?
DARKNESS CREPT IN THE SHADOWS -
HOW DID HE ESCAPE OUR MURDEROUS ONSLAUGHT
UPON THE POOR SLAVES OF
ISRAEL?
ONE DAY AT HIGH NOON -
A CROWD OF PEOPLE, YOUNG AND OLD GATHERED
WITH PALM LEAVES -
HOW THEY SHOUTED WITH JOY -
FOR THERE ON A YOUNG DONKEY COLT -
THEY PROCLAIMED HIM THEIR KING!
"HOSANNA! HOSANNA! HAIL TO OUR KING!"
WHAT A JOYOUS CELEBRATION THIS DAY WAS FOR
THE CHILDREN OF ISRAEL!
WHAT A DREADFUL DAY OF DOOM WAS FOR THE
CRUEL ROMAN MASTERS!

OH! JERUSALEM!
OH! JERUSALEM!
LET YOUR TEARS MINGLE WITH THE TEARS OF YOUR
HEAVENLY FATHER -
IN THE ROLLING THUNDER -
HEAR HIS ANGUISHED CRY!
FOR THERE UPON A HILL CALLED GOLGOTHA -
HIS BELOVED SON HUNG UPON A CROSS!
DO YOU HEAR DARKNESS LAUGH IN GLEE?

CAN YOU SEE THE CRUEL MASTERS OF ROME RAISE
THEIR CHALICES OF WINE IN VICTORY!

DO NOT CRY, LITTLE ONE -
FOR THIS STORY IS A STORY OF LOVE, A STORY OF
HOPE -
FOR THIS BEGAN IN A LITTLE TOWN OF BETHLEHEM -
THOUGH IT SEEMED THIS STORY CAME TO A TRAGIC
END -
YET -
DOWN THROUGH THE JOURNALS OF HISTORY -
OUR MESSIAH STILL LIVES ON IN THE HEARTS OF HIS
FATHER'S CHILDREN -
HIS GIFT OF LOVE -
IS OUR VICTORY OVER THE DARK CRUEL MASTERS -
DEATH HAS NO HOLD ON THOSE WHO OUR HEAVENLY
FATHER BESTOWED HIS WONDROUS GIFT OF LIFE!

(*Footnote)
Praise the Lord! Started this 12/5/94 at 8:30 A.M., finished at
11:55 A.M. intermittently at work!

CRY IN THE NIGHT

BENEATH THE BLACK STARRY NIGHT -
A SINGLE CRY BREAKS THE SILENCE!
AND THE PAGES OF MAN'S HISTORY WERE TORN ASUN-
DER!
CELESTIAL BEINGS OF GLORIOUS HARMONIES
ANNOUNCED THE BIRTH OF A KING!
SHEPHERDS WITH SLEEP CLOUDED EYES -
LOOKED INTO THE BLACK STARRY NIGHT -
A SINGLE STAR GLOWED WITH AN INTENSE LIGHT -
ILLUMINATING IN SHADOWS THE VERDANT SHEP-
HERDS PASTURE!
NEIGHBORING SHEPHERDS GATHERED IN SILENT AWE -
WONDERING WHAT MIGHTY KING WAS BORN THAT
COMMANDED SUCH A MIGHTY ANGELIC CHORUS!
THEY MURMURED AMONGST THEMSELVES -
"WHAT MAGNIFICENCE!"
"THIS NEWBORN KING MUST BE KING ABOVE ALL
KINGS!"
"COME, LET US GO AND SEE THIS BABE AND GIVE HIM
HOMAGE!"
BY THE GUIDING STAR UP ABOVE -
THEY FOLLOWED IT'S SILVERY PATH -
NOT TO A PHAROAH'S HOME -
NOT TO A KING'S COURT -
BUT TO AN INNKEEPER'S BARNSTALL!
THERE IN THE COMPANY OF COWS,GOATS AND DON-
KEYS -
THE STAR SHONE UPON THE THATCHED ROOF -
AND THROUGH THE CRACKS, THE SILVERY RAYS
ENGULFED THE THREESOME -

THE BABE'S MOTHER -
THE BABE'S FATHER -
THE WONDROUS BABY KING!
HOW THE ANGELIC HOSTS SANG IN SWEET MELODY A
LULLABYE OF PRAISE TO THEIR KING!
AND IN THE SHEPHERDS HEARTS, THEY KNEW THIS
WAS NO ORDINARY BABE -
THIS WAS GOD ON EARTH!
THIS WAS GOD'S BABY!
WITH TREMBLING KNEES THEY KNELT DOWN BEFORE
THE BABE IN THE IN THE MANGER -
THE ONLY GIFT THEY COULD GIVE WAS THEIR ADORA-
TION AND LOVE -

FOR THIS BABY'S CRY, THIS CHILD BORN IN THE STILL-
NESS OF THE NIGHT -
TORE THE PAGES OF MEN'S IMAGINATIONS AND
BRANDED THE SHEPHERDS HEARTS WITH A REVELA-
TION SO AWESOME -
THEY HEARD THE ANGELIC HOST PROCLAIM:
"THIS IS EMMANUEL -
GOD IS WITH YOU!"
"THIS IS THE LORD OF ALL CREATION!" "PEACE BE
UNTO ALL MEN -
"FOR THIS NIGHT A KING IS BORNE UNTO YOU!"

BENEATH THE BLACK STARRY NIGHT -
A SINGLE CRY BREAKS THE SILENCE -
"OH! MY FATHER! LET THIS CUP PASS BY ME!"
"YET -
"LET YOUR WILL BE DONE NOT MINE!"
A WORN AND WEARY FIGURE KNELT BESIDE AN OVER-
TURNED STONE OF COLD GRANITE -
HANDS SO FINE AND DELICATE,
YET, FIRM AND STURDY TO BRACE THE CHALICE OF
REDEMPTION CLASPED TOGETHER SO TIGHTLY -

HEAD BENT TO THE COLDNESS OF THE IMMOVABLE
STONE -
A TREMBLING SIGH INTO THE MISTS OF PRE-DAWN -
TEARS OF MOLTEN LAVA FLOWED FROM THE STEEL
FRAME OF HIS DETERMINED VISAGE -
HIS HAIR GLISTENED IN THE STARRY NIGHT -
EVEN THE STARS CRIED WITH THIS SILENT SOLITARY
MAN OF GRIEF AND SORROWS -
THEIR SILVERY TEARDROPS UPON HIS CROWN -
THIS IS THEIR KING -
THIS IS THEIR LORD!

BENEATH THE BLACKENED STORM-FILLED SKY -
A CRY TORE ASUNDER THE VEILS OF HEAVEN -
"FATHER!"
"FATHER!"
"WHY HAST THOU FORSAKEN ME!"
AND IN REPLY -
THE BLACKENED CLOUDS RUMBLED AND SHOOK THE
EARTH AND THE FIRMAMENT!
BOLTS OF LIGHTENING STRUCK THE DRY DUST-FILLED
EARTH!
PELTS OF COLD RAIN LASHED ACROSS THE MOCKING
JEERING CROWD!
THE BEREAVED BELOVED FRIENDS OF THIS LONE
TRANS-CRUCIFIED KING HUDDLED AND MOANED
THEIR LOSS!
THEIR HEARTS TORN ASUNDER BY THE ANGRY ELE-
MENTS -
WIND TORE AT THEIR BENT BODIES -
STONES OF ICY COLD RAIN PELTED THEIR SOAKEN
BONES -
THE GROUND TORE ITSELF IN GRIEF TO SEE IT'S
MIGHTY LORD SO CRUELLY TORTURED AND SHAMED
HANGING THERE UPON A DEADENED TRUNK OF A
CURSED TREE!

AGAIN A SINGLE CRY TORE ACROSS THE CHAOS -
"FATHER!"

"FORGIVE THEM!"
"THEY DO NOT KNOW WHAT THEY HAVE DONE!"
EYES OF STILL BLUE WATERS TRANSFIXED UPON THE
HEAVENS -
WITH A SIGH OF RELIEF -
HE PROCLAIMED TO THE HEAVENS -
HE PROCLAIMED TO THE WORLD -
                    "IT IS FINISHED!"
A FINAL SHUDDER -
HIS MAGNIFICENT SPIRIT BROKE FREE FROM THE TOR-
TURED HUMAN SHELL -
THE KING -
EMMANUEL -
BEGAN HIS JOURNEY HOME TO HIS BELOVED FATHER!

NOW, IN THE MISTS OF TIME -
A SINGLE CRY TEARS THE VEILS OF HEAVEN ASUNDER -
A CRUSHED AND WOUNDED HEART CRIES OUT -
"LORD! WHY HAST THOU ABANDONED ME?"
"LORD! WHY HAST THOU DEPARTED AND LEFT ME IN
THIS WORLD THAT IS DARK WITH THE FIERCE BAT-
TLES OF HATRED AND DEATH SURROUNDING ME?"
"LORD! YOU PROMISED YOU WILL NEVER LEAVE ME!"
A GRIEVING, KNEELING LONELY FIGURE SILENTLY
CRIES OUT IN THE STILLNESS OF TIME -
A HUSHED EXPECTEDNESS FILLS THE EMPTY VOID OF
HIS HEART'S CHAMBERS -
A FIRM, YET, TENDER KNOCKING SOUNDS ON THE
STONEY DOOR -
THE MASTER'S VOICE CALLS -
"SON - HERE I AM!"
"WILL YOU LET ME LIVE HERE IN THE CHAMBERS OF
YOUR EMPTY HEART?"

"WILL YOU LET ME FILL YOU WITH JOY AND GLAD-
NESS?"
SUDDENLY!
THE BEREAVED SHADOW OF A BEING -
JUMPS UP AND WITH JOYOUS SHOUTS -
THE MISTS OF DESPAIR VANISH! THE GLORY OF HIS
LORD SURROUNDS HIM -
HE SEES THAT HE IS ON A MAJESTIC MOUNTAIN TOP -
NOT IN THE GLOOMY SHADOW-FILLED VALLEY
BELOW -
DEATH IS NOT STALKING HIM -
BUT BESIDE HIM -
IN ALL HIS KINGLY GLORY -
STOOD -
EMMANUEL -
GOD IS WITH ME!

(*Footnote)
Praise and glory to the Lord! Started this on 9/20/93 at 10:30
A.M., finished this at 3:15
P.M. (Had a two hour interruption)praise the Lord!

PROPHECY 7/8/94

MY BELOVED -
COME!
LET US COME TOGETHER -
BELOVED -
THE TEMPEST IS RAGING!
THE OCEAN SWELLS ARE OVERWHELMING THE
SHORES OF YOUR FAITH!
YET -
FEAR NOT, MY BELOVED!
I AM YOUR ANCHOR!
NO WINDS OF CHANGE CAN TEAR YOU AWAY FROM
ME!
NO GALE FORCES CAN SWEEP YOU OFF THE COURSE I
HAVE PLACED YOUR FEET UPON!
NO FIERY BOLTS OF THE ENEMY'S HATRED CAN BEND
YOU OR SWAY YOU AWAY FROM ME!
FOR MY BELOVED -
I AM HOLDING ONTO YOU!
MY LOVE IS SO GREAT -
I WATCH OVER YOU WITH A JEALOUS GUARDING -
THY ENEMIES ARE MINE -
KNOW THAT EVEN IN THE DARKEST PART OF THE DEL-
UGE OF DESPAIR -
CAN YOU BE WRESTLED FROM ME!
SO, COME, MY BELOVED -
SIT BY MY SIDE -
HERE IN THIS SECRET GARDEN -
ALL IS CALM!
FOR MY PEACE IS ABIDING WITHIN YOU AND ALL
AROUND YOU, MY BELOVED!

SEE WITH YOUR FATHER'S EYES -
HEAVENLY LEGIONS OF WARRIORS AND I AS YOUR
KING,
WE SHALL STAND ON THE VICTORY OF CALVARY!
SEE THYSELVES CLOTHED IN GARMENTS AS DEEPLY
CRIMSON -
YET -
THERE BENEATH -
LIES THE GARMENTS OF MY BRIDE!

YES! BELOVED -
BELOVED -
YOU ARE MY BELOVED BRIDE -
I AM YOUR BRIDEGROOM!
SO COME -
FEAST DEEPLY OF MY LOVE!
THEN BELOVED -
POUR OUT THE NEW WINE TO THE GUESTS THAT I
HAVE CALLED TO JOIN US!
WASH THEIR DUSTY FEET -
CLOTHE THEM IN SOFT WHITE LINEN GARMENTS -
AND YOU SHALL BE MY CROWN OF GLORY FOR ALL TO
SEE -
WHAT A MIGHTY GOD YOU SERVE LOVINGLY AND
WILLINGLY!
LET MY JOY BE YOUR STRENGTH -
LET MY LOVE BE YOUR COVERING WHERE THE
ENEMY HAS WOUNDED YOU!
SO, COME!
SIT BY ME!
LET US TOGETHER SING SONGS OF PRAISE AND VICTO-
RY -
NOW IN THIS DEEP DARK HOUR!

(*Footnote)
Praise the Lord! Received this on July 8,1994.

REACHING FOR THE STARS!

DID YOU EVER NOTICE THAT ON A MIDNIGHT CLEAR
SKY THE STARS SHINE WITH A FIERY SPARKLE -
THEY SEEM TO BE DIAMONDS TOSSED UPON A VEL-
VETY CANVAS BY A DIAMOND MERCHANT SHOWING
HIS TREASURES!
AND HOW OFTEN DO WE STRETCH ON OUR TIP-TOES
TOWARDS THE HEAVENS -
DESIRING WITH ALL OF OUR HEARTS -
TO JUST TOUCH ONE STELLAR GEM!
SO, TOO, WE DESIRE TO TOUCH OUR LOVED ONES -
YET -
THEY SEEM JUST AS FAR OFF AS THOSE SPARKLING
DIAMONDS UP ABOVE!
SO CLOSE -
YET -
SO FAR AWAY TOUCHABLE -
YET -
UNTOUCHABLE!

HOW OFTEN DO WE HEAR AND SING THAT ETERNAL
CHRISTMAS MELODY:
"UPON A MIDNIGHT CLEAR, THE ANGELS PROCLAIM-
ING: "PEACE ON ALL THE EARTH!"
AND FOR A BRIEF MOMENT IN TIME -
WE SEE ONE ANOTHER AS BRILLIANT JEWELS OF
LOVE, HOPE, PEACE,
COMPASSION AND JOY!
TIL -
IN THE BRIGHT DAWN OF REALITY BEARS DOWN UPON
US -

THERE IS NO LOVE -
ONLY HATRED!
THERE IS NO HOPE -
ONLY DESPERATION!
THERE IS NO PEACE -
ONLY RAGE AND BITTERNESS!
THERE IS NO COMPASSION -
ONLY AN INDIFFERENCE TO ONE'S UNFORTUNATE
PLIGHT OF LIFE!
AND...JOY -
ONLY IN THAT ONE BRIEF MOMENT ON BATED BREATH -
ON OUR TIPPY-TOES -
ARMS STRETCHED TO THAT MIDNIGHT VELVETY
CANVAS,
WHERE OUR TREASURES OF THE HEART TANTALIZING
US WITH PROMISES OF HOPE!

YET -
FROM THE VERY HEAVENS THAT SEEM SO CLOSE,
YET -
SO UNATTAINABLE -
A MESSIAH CAME DOWN TO HIS BELOVED FATHER'S
CHILDREN -
A BABE BORN ONLY TO LAY DOWN HIS LIFE -
THE GREATEST GIFT OF LOVE -
LOVINGLY FROM OUR FATHER'S HEART -
HE GAVE HIS BELOVED TREASURE CHEST FILLED TO
OVERFLOWING WITH HIS JEWELS OF LIFE -
CONTAINED DEEPLY WITHIN HIS ONLY BEGOTTEN SON -
OUR SAVIOR -
OUR DELIVERER -
OUR YASHUA HAMASHIA -
JESUS CHRIST OF NAZARETH!

SO LOOK UP!

SEE THAT BRILLIANT PULSING STAR -
THERE BETWEEN THE HEAVENS AND THE HORIZON OF
OUR LIVES, YES -
THE STAR THAT BECKONED THREE WISE MEN TO A
MANGER'S COVE -
WHERE THE LUMINESCENCE OF GOD SHONE IN A
BABE WRAPPED IN SWADDLING CLOTH!
NOW -
WE CAN TOUCH THE STARS -
NOW -
WE CAN LOVE AS THE 'CARPENTER'S! SON LOVED US -
FOR HIS LOVE WAS NOT OF THIS SHADOWY EARTH -
BUT FROM THE VERY HEART OF HIS FATHER -
WHO -
BY HIS LAYING DOWN HIS LIFE -
WE ARE ANCHORED DEEPLY INTO THE BEDROCK OF
GOD'S SOVEREIGN LOVE!

SEE, BELOVED!
DEEP WITHIN YOU -
SEE THE MIDNIGHT CANVAS OF YOUR HEART -
ALL TORN AND WORN AND FADED -
NOW -

SEE THE FATHER, THRU HIS BELOVED SON -
THE MANY STARS OF LOVE, HOPE, PEACE, COMPAS-
SION AND JOY -
YES -
WE ARE IN AND WITH AND THRU JESUS -
ABBA FATHER'S DIAMONDS SCATTERED UPON THE
BLACK VOID OF THE ENEMY'S CAMP -
WHERE THE LOST, THE IMPRISONED, THE WOUNDED,
THE DELUDED CHILDREN OF THE MOST HIGH GOD -
CAN STRETCH FORTH THEIR SPIRIT ARMS TOWARDS
THE HEAVENS -
AND RECEIVE THEIR PORTION OF THEIR INHERITANCE

WITH JESUS -
THE GREATEST GIFT -
ETERNAL LIFE!
NEVER TO SHED ANOTHER TEAR, NEVER TO WALK
MAIMED, NEVER TO BE BLINDED -
FOR WE ARE NOW THE FIERY DIAMONDS OF HOPE IN
THIS MIDNIGHT HOUR!

(*Footnote)
Started this 9/29/94 at 8:30 A.M. Finished this at 9:00 A.M.
Praise the Lord!

PROPHECY 7/23/92

OH! WHO WILL HEAR MY WORD?
OH! WHO WILL FOLLOW THE WIND OF MY HOLY SPIR-
IT?
OH! WHO WILL WATCH DURING THE NIGHT SEASONS?
WILL THERE BE A WATCHMAN IN THE TOWER?
WHO WILL SOUND THE TRUMPET OF WARNING FOR
THE ENEMY IS NEIGH APPROACHING!
YET - FEAR NOT!
FOR I AM THE WARRIOR!
FOR I AM THE KING OF ALL KINGS!
I COME TO BRING FORTH MY BRIDE!
ARE YOU READY, MY BELOVED?
HAVE YOU PUT ON YOUR BEAUTIFUL GARMENTS OF
WHITE?
ARE YOU ADORNED WITH THE NECKLACES OF GOLD
AND SILVER?

COME, OH YE PRIESTS OF THE NATIONS -
SOUND THE TRUMPETS!
COME SINGING, COME DANCING WITH MANY INSTRU-
MENTS -
FOR I AM DELIGHTED!
I AM HERE IN THE MIDST OF THIS JUBILEE!

SO, COME, BELOVED -
BE MY VOICE, BE MY HEART!
I NEED YOU SO MUCH -
FOR MANY ARE LOST -
MANY ARE IN NEED!
COME, IT IS TIME FOR THE HARVEST!

THE WIND'S VOICE

ALL ACROSS THE LAND, A WIND IS BLOWING!
CAN YOU HEAR HIS VOICE?
ALL ACROSS THE LAND, THERE IS A RUSTLING OF
VOICES -
CAN YOU HEAR THEM?
IF YOU BE STILL -
YOU CAN HEAR THE CREATOR'S VOICE!
IF YOU BE STILL -
YOU CAN HEAR THE ANGRY SNARLS OF THE WOLVES!
IF YOU BE STILL -
YOU CAN HEAR THE CRIES OF THE PEOPLE!
IF YOU FEEL THE WIND BLOWING ACROSS THE LAND-
SCAPE OF YOUR HEART -
WHO IS THE WIND?

SHOULD THE WIND BE A HOWLING STORM -
WHIPPING AT THE VERY ROOTS OF YOUR FAITH -
SHOULD YOU RAISE YOUR FEARS INTO THE GALE -
DO YOU BELIEVE SOMEONE IS LISTENING?

SHOULD THE WIND BE A TEARING TORNADO -
RIPPING THROUGH THE VERY FIBERS OF YOUR SOUL -
WHOSE TONGUES ARE LASHING AT YOUR INNOCENCE?

SHOULD THE WIND BE A GENTLE, COOL, REFRESHING
BREEZE -
BLOWING IN THE GARDENS OF YOUR HEART -
WHO IS THE GARDENER WITH HIS HEALING TOUCH TO
STRENGTHEN YOU EACH TIME AN ILL WIND BLOWS?

HEAR ME, MY BELOVED!
THERE ARE MANY WINDS BLOWING IN THIS LAND!
THERE ARE MANY STORMS THAT WOULD TEAR YOU
AWAY FROM ME!
YET -
FEAR NOT!
FOR THERE IS NOTHING IN HEAVEN, ON THE EARTH,
OR BENEATH THE EARTH THAT CAN SNATCH THEE
AWAY FROM ME!
GREAT IS MY LOVE FOR THEE, MY PRECIOUS!
THAT I HAVE GIVEN YOU MY ONLY BEGOTTEN SON!
COULD YOU BE AS ABRAHAM AND SACRIFICE YOUR
ONLY BELOVED CHILD?
HEAR MY VOICE!
IT IS SOFT, GENTLE AS A REFRESHING BREEZE IN YOUR
HEART -
NOT THE TEARING, WHIPPING STORMS OF OUR ENEMIES -
YES, BELOVED -
THY ENEMIES ARE MINE!
SO, FEAR NOT!
COME TO CALVARY, THERE IS THE DOOR OF EVER-
LASTING LIFE -
THERE YOU WILL BE REFRESHED FROM THE STORMS
OF THIS MOMENTARY LIFE -
FOR IN A TWINKLING OF AN EYE -
WE SHALL SEE ONE ANOTHER CLEARLY!
THERE WILL NO LONGER BE ANY DARK MIRROR TO
LOOK THROUGH -
FOR YOU SHALL RECEIVE A NEW GLORIOUS BEING -
THE TRUE IMAGE OF THY CREATOR!
YES, BELOVED, I AM HE WHO HAS CREATED THEE IN
MY LIKENESS!
I HAVE CALLED YOU FROM THE VERY DEPTHS OF THE
SEA -
HAVE YOU HEARD MY VOICE IN THE WIND?
HAVE YOU FELT MY HOLY SPIRIT'S REFRESHING

BREEZE IN THY WEARY HEART?
COME!
LAY DOWN YOUR BURDENS AT THE FOOT OF THE
CROSS OF THY VICTORY!
BOUGHT AT THE HIGHEST PRICE -
MY ONLY BEGOTTEN SON'S SHED BLOOD!
BY HIS REDEEMING BLOOD, I HAVE RANSOMED THEE
FROM THE ADVERSARY!
SO GREAT IS HIS HATRED FOR ME, THAT WHEN HE SEES
MY SON'S IMAGE MIRRORED IN THEE -
HIS FURIOUS HOT ILL WIND BLOWS ACROSS THE
WILDERNESS OF THY SOUL -
BUT COME TO ME, MY PRECIOUS LITTLE ONE!
FOR AS THY FATHER -
I WILL NOT ALLOW ANY HARM TO BEFALL YOU, ONLY
THAT WHICH I ALLOW MY ENEMY TO TEST YOU, FOR
IN THE FASHIONING OF A MIGHTY WEAPON, THE
METAL MUST BE TRIED!
EACH TIME THE METAL INTENSIFIES IT'S SHARPNESS
TO PIERCE THE ENEMY'S HEART!
SO, TOO, I FASHION THEE!
ART THOU WILLING, MY BELOVED?
FOR MANY ARE THE VOICES OF MY PEOPLE CRYING
OUT FOR THE TOUCH OF A COOL REFRESHING BREEZE!
YES! BELOVED! WITH MY HOLY SPIRIT ABIDING WITH-
IN THEE WITH MY GARDEN OF LIFE WITHIN THEE -
MANY A PRECIOUS LITTLE ONE WILL SAVOR THE
SWEETNESS OF MY HEALING ABUNDANT EVERLAST-
ING LIFE WITHIN THEM!
SO, LISTEN, MY BELOVED, TO THE WIND -
BEND AS A REED -
FEAR NOT -
YOU SHALL NOT BE BRUISED OR BROKEN -
YET -
YOU SHALL BE A REFUGE FOR THE LOST,
A HEALING OASIS FOR THE THIRSTY SOULS!

BE STILL, BELOVED -
FOR I AM THE LORD THY GOD!

(*Footnote)
Started this at 4:10 P.M., finished this at 4:40 P.M. Praise the
Lord! Great are thee, my Lord! Hallelujah!

PROPHECY 1/27/93

HEAR ME, MY BELOVED!
HEAR MY VOICE!
IT IS IN THE CHANGING TIDE -
IT IS IN THE CHANGING WIND -
IT IS IN THE MOURNING COO OF A DOVE!
YES, MY BELOVED,
MY HOLY SPIRIT IS GRIEVING -
FOR OUR ENEMY ROAMS TO AND FRO IN THIS LAND,
HE IS SEEKING THE WEAK, THE LOST, THE WOUNDED
CHILDREN!
SO, MY BELOVED -
GO FORWARD -
EVER FORWARD -
LET MY HOLY SPIRIT GUIDE YOU THROUGH THE NAR-
ROW PATH!
YES, MY BELOVED,
THE PATH IS NARROW,
THE RICH SEARCHED FOR THE GATE TO ETERNITY -
YET -
WHEN THE GATE STOOD IN FRONT AND INSTRUCTED
THAT THE YOUNG MAN GIVE TO THE POOR ALL HIS
WEALTH -
HE COULD NOT!
IT IS EASIER FOR A CAMEL TO PASS THROUGH THE EYE
OF THE NEEDLE!
SO, MY BELOVED,
LOVE ONE ANOTHER -
LET YOUR VOICE BE MY VOICE -
LET YOUR LOVE BE MY LOVE -
FOR LOVE IS THE GREATEST HEALER -

THE SWORD IS NOT MIGHTY -
BUT LOVE TURNETH HATE -
HATE BECOMES LOVE -
THEN HEALING BECOMES THE WORDS OF MY FATHER!
FOR WE ARE LOVE -
NO GREATER LOVE IS THERE -
THEN LOVE THAT REQUIRES NOTHING -
BUT SIMPLY AN EMBRACE OF HOPE!
SO, COME!
FOLLOW ME!

I COPIED THIS FROM A BOOK CALLED:" STREAMS IN
THE DESERT II
BY MRS. CHARLES E. COWMAN.
JANUARY 5 _____

......CALLED TO BE SAINTS:......(ROM. 1:17; 1 COR. 1:2).

WHY WERE THE SAINTS, SAINTS?
IT IS QUITE SIMPLE.

BECAUSE THEY WERE "CHEERFUL" WHEN IT WAS DIF-
FICULT TO BE CHEERFUL.
BECAUSE THEY WERE "PATIENT" WHEN IT WAS DIFFI-
CULT TO BE PATIENT.
BECAUSE THEY PUSHED ON WHEN THEY WANTED TO
STAND STILL.
BECAUSE THEY KEPT SILENT WHEN THEY WANTED TO
TALK.
BECAUSE THEY WERE AGREEABLE WHEN THEY
WANTED TO BE DISAGREEABLE.

SELECTED

WHAT IS A SAINT?
THAT WAS ALL!

A *JEWEL* IN DISGUISE,
A *PRINCE* IN PEASANT'S GARBS.
AN IMMORTAL *LIFE* IN DYING FLESH.
AN *AMBASSADOR* OF THE KING ETERNAL, DETAINED
ON FOREIGN SOIL.
A *MONARCH* AT THE FOOT OF THE THRONE, WAITING
FOR HIS CROWN.

A ROYAL SLAVE IN A PRISON OF CLAY, PREPARING FOR A MANSION.

A *TRAVELER* ON A ROCKY ROAD, BOUND FOR THE STREETS OF GOLD.

A *WATCHMAN* ON THE MIDNIGHT HILLS, TO GREET THE EVERLASTING DAY.

A *DIAMOND* IN THE ROUGH, BEING POLISHED TO SHINE AS THE STARS.

A *NUGGET* OF GOLD IN THE CRUCIBLE, TO BE REFINED FROM ITS DROSS.

A *PEARL* IN THE OYSTER, TO BE DELIVERED FROM THE BODY OF FLESH.

A *LAMP* IN A DARK NIGHT, SOON TO BLAZE FORTH WITH EVERLASTING LIGHT.

A *STRANGER* IN THE MIDST OF ENEMIES, HURRYING ON TO LIVE IN EVERLASTING FELLOWSHIP.

A *FLOWER* IN A GARDEN OF BRIARS, SOON TO UNFOLD ITS PETALS WHERE THE *ROSE OF SHARON* BLOOMS.

UNKNOWN

LOVER OF MY SOUL

MY SECRET PLACE

COME!
COME INTO THE SECRET PLACE -
FOR THERE IS MUCH I WOULD LIKE TO SPEAK TO YOU!
SEE! MY BELOVED!
AS YOU AWAKEN -
THE ENEMY TREMBLES,
FOR I'VE CALLED YOU FROM THE DEPTHS OF THE SEA!
YEA!
BELOVED -
SO GREAT IS MY LOVE FOR THEE, MY BELOVED -
THAT I STAND AT THE DOOR INTO LIFE EVERLASTING!
THIS BELOVED -
IS YOURS, THIS MOMENT -
NOT TOMORROW -
BUT THIS MOMENT!
FOR AS YOU ABIDE IN ME -
I TOO, BELOVED, SHALL ABIDE IN THEE!
COME, BELOVED!
BE STILL,
HEAR MY VOICE IN THE QUIET -
AS A LOVER WHISPERS TO HIS BELOVED -
I WHISPER TO YOU -
COME, LEARN OF ME, FOR I AM HERE!

LIGHT OF JESUS OF NAZARETH!

HAVE YOU EVER LOOKED AROUND AT ONE ANOTHER?
HAVE YOU EVER LOOKED DEEPLY IN THEIR EYES?
THERE ARE PEOPLE WHO BECOME NERVOUS -
THERE ARE PEOPLE WHO BECOME SHY AND TIMID -
THERE ARE PEOPLE WHO WILL LOOK DEEPLY IN YOUR
EYES AND SWEAR THE MOON WAS BLUE WHEN YOU
AND I KNOW THE MOON IS WHITE OR YELLOW!

HAVE YOU EVER LOOKED AROUND AT ONE ANOTHER?
HAVE YOU EVER HUNGRILY LOOKED FOR SOMEONE
TO LOOK BACK AT YOU FOR LOVE AND COMFORT?
THERE ARE PEOPLE WHO WILL LOOK WITH EYES
PLEADING FOR LOVE -
THERE ARE PEOPLE WHO WILL LOOK WITH EYES
PLEADING FOR COMFORT IN THEIR LONELINESS -
THERE ARE EYES FROM SUCH CUNNING LIARS WHO
PROMISE TO LOVE AND CHERISH YOU -
BUT -
DON'T TURN YOUR BACK -
FOR THEY WILL UTTER THE SAME EMPTY PROMISES
TO ANOTHER BEGGING SOUL!

HAVE YOU EVER LOOKED INTO THE EYES OF ONE WHO
DIES ON A CROSS?
HAVE YOU EVER LOOKED INTO THE EYES OF ONE WHO
LOVES YOU DESPITE YOURSELF?
HAVE YOU EVER LOOKED INTO THE EYES OF ONE WHO
CARES FOR YOU DESPITE THE CHAOTIC WORLD YOU
ARE IN?

HAVE YOU EVER SEEN SUCH EYES SO FULL OF LOVE, TENDERNESS AND COMPASSION FOR YOU?

LOOK DEEPLY INTO MY EYES -
THERE YOU WILL SEE THE LIGHT AND JOY OF MY HEART!
LOOK DEEPLY INTO MY EYES -
THERE YOU WILL SEE THE LIGHT AND JOY OF MY LIFE!
THERE YOU WILL SEE MY ONLY TRUE, LOYAL AND FAITHFUL FRIEND!
THERE LOOKING BACK AT YOU WITH ALL OF HIS TENDER LOVE, GLORIOUS LIFE,
AND BUBBLING JOY -
IS -
JESUS, LORD OF MY LIFE!
JESUS, KING OF MY SOUL!
FOR ONLY THE LIFE OF JESUS INFUSED IN MY BEING BY THE POWER OF THE HOLY SPIRIT -
CAN MY EYES SHINE FORTH HIS LOVE FOR YOU!
FOR ONLY JESUS IS STEADFAST, TRUSTWORTHY AND EVER FAITHFUL -
DESPITE - OUR SHABBY SELVES -
DESPITE - OUR TORN IMAGES OF OURSELVES -
DESPITE - OUR FAILURES, OUR LOST DREAMS!
FOR THE LIGHT AND JOY OF JESUS IS SHINING THROUGH MY HEART AND SOUL!
TO BLESS YOU -
TO SAVE YOU FROM THE DEEP DARKNESS OF DESPAIR!
SO, COME!
LET US ALL COME TOGETHER AS ONE IN PURPOSE -
LET US BE THE PURE BRIDE -
BLUSHING IN JOY -
FOR OUR BRIDEGROOM HAS COME TO CLAIM HIS OWN TRUE BRIDE!
WHOSE EYES ARE BRIGHT AS STARS -
WHOSE EYES ARE DANCING IN THE LIGHT OF GOD'S TRUTH -

THAT DEEP WITHIN MY EYES -
YOU WILL SEE MY LOVER'S LIGHT AND JOY SHINING
FORTH AS A BRILLIANT BEACON OF HOPE!

(*Footnote)
Praise the Lord! Received this on 8/10/90. Started this at 11:10
P.M. Finished this at I 1:35 P. M. Praise God!

PROPHECY 7/25/92

MY BELOVED!
DO YOU KNOW HOW GREAT MY LOVE IS FOR THEE?
LIFE -
MY LIFE WAS GIVEN AND IS GIVEN UNTO YOU -
DAILY, MOMENT INTO THE NEXT MOMENT -
UNENDING LOVE -
LOVE THAT CONSUMES SELF-LOVE -
LOVE THAT CONSUMES THE POWER OF OUR ENEMY'S
HATE!

SO, MY BELOVED -
I AM YOUR LOVER -
YES -
I AM THE LOVER OF YOUR SOUL!
YES -
I AM YOUR PRINCE OF PEACE -
PEACE, MY BELOVED -
CONTENTMENT, THAT NO STORM CAN OVERTAKE YOU -
NO FLOOD CAN SWEEP YOU AWAY -
FOR I AM YOUR ANCHOR -
I AM YOUR DELIVERER AND PROTECTOR -
I AM ALL, ALL, THAT YOU NEED -
MY LIFE, IS YOUR LIFE -
WILL YOU OFFER YOUR LIFE TO ME?
WILL YOU OPEN THE DOOR OF YOUR HEART TO ME?
SO, COME!
LET MY LOVE BE YOUR SHIELD IN THIS DARKENED
WORLD -
FOR I AM LIGHT!
I AM LOVE!
I AM YOUR AUTHOR OF FAITH TO GO ON!

PROPHECY OF 9/18/94

ARISE!
AWAKE MY PRECIOUS CHILD!
FOR IT IS DANGEROUS TO SLEEP!
FOR THE WOLVES AND THE YOUNG LIONS ARE ROAM-
ING ABOUT SEEKING WHOM THEY MAY DEVOUR -
BUT, FEAR NOT!
BELOVED!
MY HOLY SPIRIT IS BESIDE YOU -
ALL. AROUND YOU ARE MY WARRIOR ANGELS!
SO, AWAKE, PRECIOUS!
IT IS TIME TO CLEANSE MY HOUSE -
FOR SOON THE MASTER IS RETURNING!
ARE YOU READY FOR HIS RETURN?
LET ME HELP YOU REMOVE THE COBWEBS OF UNFOR-
GIVENESS!
LET ME BLOW THE DUST OF BITTER MEMORIES AWAY!
WOULD YOU ALLOW ME TO BE COMPLETE LORD AND
MASTER OF YOUR HOUSE?
OR WILL YOU ONLY ALLOW ME TO BE LORD OF A FEW
CHAMBERS?
HOW LONG WILL YOU ALLOW THE STRONGMAN TO
RESIDE DEEPLY IN YOU?
HOW LONG WILL YOU ALLOW HIM TO ROB AND STEAL
FROM YOU?
CAN DARKNESS HAVE FELLOWSHIP WITH LIGHT?
CAN LIGHT ABIDE WITH DARKNESS?
EITHER THERE WILL BE TOTAL LIGHT OR TOTAL DARK-
NESS!

PRECIOUS LITTLE ONE -
YOU MUST CHOOSE NOW!
EITHER YOU COME TO CALVARY -
AND RECEIVE THE LORD OF YOUR SOUL TO BE KING
ABOVE ALL KINGS IN YOUR HEART!
WILL YOU BE CLEANSED IN THE SHED BLOOD OF MY
HOLY LAMB?
PRECIOUS LITTLE ONE!
I HAVE GIVEN YOU MY HEART -
MY ONLY BEGOTTEN SON - JESUS!
YES, BELOVED -

IN HIS NAME, THE NAME THAT HAS THE KEY OF
AUTHORITY OVER OUR ENEMIES!
YES -
BELOVED -
HE IS MY ENEMY, ALSO!
HE IS THE DESTROYER OF YOUR SOUL!
SO, PRECIOUS LITTLE ONE -
IF YOU SAW YOUR CHILD IN DANGER -
WOULD YOU NOT WARN THAT CHILD?
IF YOUR LOVED ONES WERE KIDNAPPED BY AN
ENEMY -
SO, TOO, BELOVED -
I HAVE DONE WHEN MY ENEMY LAID HOLD TO MUR-
DER MY OWN SON -
YET -
HE WILLING, NOT THE ENEMY, LAID DOWN HIS LIFE
FOR YOU!
SO, PRECIOUS -
IT'S TIME TO CLEAN AND RESTORE AND REFRESH MY
HOUSE -
FOR THE MASTER IS RETURNING -
I HAVE SENT OUT THE CALL TO COME TO THE MAR-
RIAGE FEAST!
YES!

COME, EAT FROM THE BREAD OF LIFE -
FOR IN HIM -
THERE IS LIFE!
BUT -
BEWARE, BELOVED -
IF YOU EAT OF THE ENEMY'S FEAST -
THOUGH IT LOOKS SUMPTUOUS, EVEN MORE DELI-
CIOUS THAN MINE -
THEY ARE THE FRUIT BREAD OF DEATH!
SO, PRECIOUS -
COME!
I AM HERE -
MY ARMS ARE OUTSTRETCHED TO RECEIVE YOU INTO
MY ARMS -
I AM AT THE MIDST OF THAT MOUNTAIN -
I WILL HELP YOU!
SO, ARISE!
AWAKE!
COME - MY CHILDREN -
COME INTO THE SHELTER OF MY SECRET PLACE -
LEARN OF ME -
BE DEEPLY IN DESIRE TO BE ONE WITH ME -
JUST AS MY SON PRAYED -
"FATHER -
"LET THEY BE ONE!"
DRINK DEEPLY OF THE COOL REFRESHING WATERS OF
MY WORD -
IF A WEARY TRAVELER COMES TO YOUR DOOR -
LEAD HIM TO THE MASTER OF YOUR HOUSE -
LET MY PEACE BE POOLS OF HEALING TO THE
WOUNDED ONES!
SO, COME!
IT IS TIME -
TO TAKE A STAND!
DO NOT SLUMBER ANY LONGER!
COME!

SEE THE MASTER -
YOUR BRIDEGROOM IS EVEN AT THIS MOMENT AT
YOUR DOORSTEP!

(* Footnote) Praise God! Received this on Sept. 18, 1994. This
confirmed the pastor's service!

SILENT PRAISES - SILENT VOICES

ON A DAY SO CLEAR -
ON A DAY SO FRESH -
THE BLUE SKIES CALLING -
I SING MY SONG OF PRAISES TO THE ONE ABOVE!

THOUGH YOU SEE MY ARMS SWAYING IN THE COOL
BREEZES OF THE SHORE -
THOUGH YOU SEE THE COOL GREENNESS OF MY COAT -
YET-
WITHIN ME THERE IS A NEWNESS OF LIFE!
FOR I AM A PART OF THE MAIN BRANCH OF LIFE!

THOUGH I MAY BE STONE GREY -
THOUGH I MY BE IMMOVABLE -
YET -
YOU CAN HEAR MY VOICE IN THE STILLNESS OF THE
DAY!
YET -
ALL MEN CAN HEAR MY VOICE -
THE LORD ABOVE HAS GIVEN ME A VOICE OF PRAISE!
IN THE MIGHTY BOOKS OF OLD -
I AM THERE -
SO ON THIS CLEAR DAY -
WITH ARMS RAISED HIGH TO THE HEAVENS ABOVE -
THOUGH, I BE LOWLY AND STILL -
I SING MY PRAISES TO MY LORD!

THE DOOR TO ETERNITY

AS I LAY HERE UPON MY BED, CHASING SLEEP TO
COME UPON ME -
FOR I SO LONGED TO REST AWHILE!
YET -
SLEEP WOULD ELUDE ME!
THEN SUDDENLY!
MY ROOM EXPLODED IN A BRILLIANT NOVA OF GOLD-
EN LIGHT!
MY NOSTRILS FLARED IN THE SCENT OF A GARDEN
MINGLED WITH A SWEET PUNGENT AROMA!
SWEET MELODIC VOICES FILLED MY TINY ROOM WITH
A POWERFUL VIBRANCY OF PRAISE!
THERE -
BATHED IN THE GOLDEN LIGHT -
I SAW A MAGNIFICENT PRINCE!
HIS PRESENCE FILLED MY TINY ROOM WITH HIS
GLORY!
A GOLDEN CROWN WITH CELESTIAL STARS WAS UPON
HIS HEAD!
HIS EYES BLAZED WITH A GOLDEN FIRE!
HIS SMILE WAS SO WARM AND INVITING -
HE STRETCHED FORTH HIS HAND TOWARDS ME -
HIS VOICE AS GENTLE AS THE NIGHT BREEZE, HE
SPOKE TO ME:
"COME! MY BELOVED!"
I LEAPED UP FROM MY BED AND RAN TOWARDS HIM -
"MY LORD!"
HOW TINY MY HAND WAS IN HIS BIG MUSCULAR
HAND!
YET -

I NOTICED A WOUND DEEP WITHIN IT -
I LOOKED UP AT MY KING -
IN AWE I SPOKE:
"LORD! YOUR HAND IS WOUNDED!"
"WHO HAS PIERCED YOU SO CRUELLY?"
HE SMILED SO LOVINGLY AT ME -
"SEE, MY BELOVED -
"THESE ARE WOUNDS OF LOVE-"
"FOR AS I STRETCHED OUT MY ARMS -"
"I TOOK ALL OF YOUR MORTALITY WITH ALL OF ITS
IMPERFECTIONS, WITH ALL OF ITS EVIL IMPRINTS
WITHIN YOUR SHELL OF DEATH UPON ME!"
I LOOKED AT MY LORD, NOT UNDERSTANDING HIS
WORDS OF WISDOM.
I LOOKED DOWN TO COVER MY FACE OF CONFUSION
AND I NOTICED THAT HIS FEET WERE ALSO WOUNDED!
"LORD!" I EXCLAIMED -
"THEY HAVE PIERCED YOUR FEET, ALSO!"
HIS VOICE WAS A SOFT VELVET OF COMFORT UPON ME -
"YES, MY BELOVED! FOR MY ENEMIES PLACED MY
FEET TOGETHER
"A SPIKE OF PERMANENCE WAS DRIVEN INTO THEM -
"FOR I HAVE WALKED IN YOUR PAIN -
"FOR I HAVE WALKED IN YOUR DESPAIR -
"BUT MY FOOTSTEPS BROUGHT HOPE -
"MY FOOTSTEPS BROUGHT HEALING FOR ALL THOSE
I'VE CALLED TO FOLLOW ME -
"TO WALK IN MY FOOTSTEPS -
"FOR THEY SHALL WALK INTO MY KINGDOM OF ETER-
NAL LIFE!
"WILL YOU WALK ALSO WITH ME NOW, MY BELOVED?"
HIS VOICE WAS FILLED WITH URGENCY -
I FELT HIS NEED TO FOLLOW HIM DEEP WITHIN MY
VERY BEING!
I LOOKED AT HIS WOUNDS -
AND I NOTICED THAT UPON HIS BROW, THERE WAS

PUNCTURED WOUNDS ALL AROUND HIS BEAUTIFUL HEAD!

WITH TEARS OF LOVE AND COMPASSION FOR MY LORD, I CRIED:

"LORD! WHAT HAVE THEY DONE TO YOU?"

"FEAR NOT MY BELOVED!"

"FOR MY FATHER NEEDED ME TO COME UPON THIS LAND FILLED WITH GIANTS -

"YES -

"JUST AS DAVID FACED GOLIATH, AND SLEW THE GIANT -

SO, TOO, I FACED THE GIANTS THAT HAVE ENSLAVED MY FATHER'S CHILDREN!"

"SO, I LAID ASIDE MY IMMORTALITY, AND I CLOTHED MYSELF IN YOUR IMPOVERISHED MORTAL SHELL -

"BUT DEEP WITHIN ME, MY FATHER'S WORDS OF ORDER CHURNED A RIVER OF LIFE!

"SEE HERE, MY BELOVED, THEY HAVE PIERCED MY SIDE -

"MY ENEMY NOT KNOWINGLY RELEASED THE FLOOD-GATES OF LIFE UPON THIS LAND AND UPON MY FATHER'S PEOPLE!"

"I LAID MY MORTAL BEING DOWN UPON THE TREE OF DEATH -

"YET -

"DEATH HAS BEEN PERMANENTLY VANQUISHED!

"NO LONGER WILL DEATH HAVE HIS STING UPON YOU!"

"IN LOVING OBEDIENCE TO MY FATHER'S WILL -

"I NOW WEAR A CROWN OF GLORY!"

"HERE, MY BELOVED, IS YOUR CROWN! WILL YOU BE MY BRIDE?"

"WILL YOU LAY YOUR MORTAL SELF TO BE DAILY SLAUGHTERED, SO MY PEOPLE CAN SEE MY GLORY DEEP WITHIN YOU?

"SO WE CAN STRETCH FORTH OUR ARMS OF LOVE TO

THE LOST, THE WOUNDED SOULS WANDERING AIM-
LESSLY -
"SEARCHING FOR HOPE -
"SEARCHING FOR TRUTH -
"SEARCHING FOR THAT EMPTINESS IN THEM TO BE
FILLED WITH UNSPEAKABLE JOY AND PEACE!"
I LOOKED AT MY LORD AND SAVIOR -
HIS HANDS STRETCHED FORTH IN A BECKONING WAY -
MY POOR HEART ACHED SO LONGINGLY TO CLASP HIS
DEAR TENDER HANDS -
WITH A SIGH OF LOVE SO DEEP -
I PLACED MY TINY HANDS WITHIN HIS -
AND I STEPPED THROUGH THE DOOR INTO ETERNITY!

(*Footnote)
Praise the Lord! Started this on 11/20/92 at 9:30 A.M. Finished
this at 9:45 A.M. Praise God!

THANKSGIVING TO MY GOD!

THANK YOU, ABBA FATHER, FOR ALL THE BLESSINGS AND ALLOWING ME TO REALLY KNOW YOU!
HOW YOU'VE TAKEN THIS LITTLE DEATH BLACKENED SOUL AND SHONE YOUR HOLY GLORY WITHIN!
ALL YOU ARE, BY YOUR SON'S SACRIFICE, BY THE POWER OF YOUR HOLY SPIRIT POURED IN ME!
NEVER LEAVING MY SIDE, EVEN WHEN I CRY IN PANIC AND WITH FEAR -
KINDNESS OF YOUR MERCY AND COMPASSION OVER-WHELMS ME WITH A ZEAL TO CAPTURE ALL WHO ARE LOST SUCH AS I WAS -
SOULS THAT HAVE NEVER REALLY KNOWN YOU - BY YOUR SON - WE ARE ONE!
GIVING YOU MY HEART, MY WILL, WITH LOVE SO DEEP,
I NEVER THOUGHT I COULD LOVE SO COMPLETELY -
FOR THIS IS YOUR LOVE -
EMMANUEL - GOD IS WITH US -
HIS LOVE SO GREAT -
HIS LIFE HE GAVE TO ME -
VISIONS OF YOUR MIGHTY GLORY NOT ONLY SUDDEN-LY FILLING MY WORLD -
                    BUT ALSO MY HEART!
INTO THE INNER CHAMBER, YOU HAVE BROUGHT ME TO WITNESS YOUR FIERY LOVE FOR YOUR CHILDREN -
NEAR TO YOUR HEART, YOUR MERCY AND GOODNESS UNLIMITED -
I SEE YOU STRETCHING YOUR ARMS THROUGH YOUR SON - JESUS -
SAYING: "I LOVE YOU SO MUCH!"

GOD! FORGIVE ME FOR MY WEAKNESSES!
NEVER, EVER LEAVE ME!
THANK YOU FOR YOUR PROMISES:
"SO GREAT IS MY LOVE HERE IS MY ONLY BEGOTTEN
SON - JESUS CHRIST OF NAZARETH - YOUR DELIVERER -
YOUR MESSIAH!"

WITH ALL THAT IS WITHIN ME -
YOUR LITTLE GIRL!

THE COVENANT OF LOVE GRACE AND MERCY

PROPHECY 11/1/93

COME, MY BELOVED!
LET US GO INTO THE HIGH PLACES!
FOR YEA!
THIS IS THE TIME THAT YOU MUST BE IN THE SHADOW
OF THE FATHER FOR THE LION WALKETH ABOUT FOR
WHOM HE CAN DEVOUR!
BUT - FEAR NOT!
FOR I AM WITH YOU!
REMEMBER -
THE BATTLE IS MINE!
YET -
WALK AND PRAISE IN HOLY THANKSGIVING -
FOR THE DAY OF YOUR REDEMPTION IS AT YOUR
DOORSTEP!
MY HOLY SPIRIT IS SHINING THE FATHER'S GLORY AS A
NOON DAY SUN IN THIS STORMY DARKENED NIGHT -
SO, COME! LET US BOLDLY PROCLAIM THE GOOD
NEWS TO ALL CREATION -
FOR I, YOUR KING, AM NOW AMONGST THEE!
THE ENEMY FLEES!
THE HEAVENLY HOSTS ARE REJOICING -
THE FATHER'S GLORY IS ALL AROUND THEE!
SO, COME!
BASK IN MY LOVE -
FOR LOVE HEALETH ALL WOUNDS THAT THE ENEMY
HAS INFLICTED UPON THEE!

(*Footnote) Praise the Lord! Received this prophecy on Nov. 1st,
1993 while at a Sunday service. Pastor David, allowed me to read
this to the congregation. Glory and praises to the Lord!

PROPHECY 9/21/94

MY BELOVED -
COME!
HEAR MY VOICE!
DO YOU HEAR MY VOICE IN THE WIND?
DO YOU HEAR THE VOICES OF MY CHILDREN CRYING
OUT FOR LIGHT IN THEIR DARKNESS?
BELOVED -
I HAVE PLACED THE FIRE OF MY HOLY SPIRIT DEEP
WITHIN YOU -
THOUGH YOU ARE WEAK -
AM I ALSO WEAK UNABLE TO MOVE THE MOUNTAINS
THAT WOULD KEEP YOU FROM THE PROMISED LAND -
THE LAND THAT I PROMISED YOU -
A LAND FILLED WITH MILK AND HONEY!
BUT BELOVED -
MIGHTY GIANTS ARE WITHIN THAT LAND -
YET -
FEAR NOT!
HEAR NOT THE REPORT OF THE ENEMY -
YOU COULD NOT HAVE WON THE VICTORY TO CLAIM
AND WALK IN THAT LAND!
YET -
I AS YOUR WARRIOR KING -
I AM MORE THAN ABLE TO CONQUER ALL!
DO YOU HAVE ANY GIANTS IN THE PROMISED LAND I
HAVE GIVEN TO YOU?
FEAR NOT!
I HAVE GIVEN YOU A MIGHTY WARRIOR - JESUS -
YES!
BELOVED -

IN THAT NAME ALONE -
ALL OF HEAVEN -
ALL OF THE EARTH -
ALL BENEATH THE EARTH WILL TREMBLE!
SEE -
HE COMES WITH HIS ANGELIC WARRIORS!
SEE -
JUST AS ELIJAH SPOKE WITH ELISHA -
LOOK NOT THROUGH THE EYE OF THE ENEMY -
SEE -
WITH THE EYES OF FAITH!
FOR BELOVED -
WITH A TINY MUSTARD SEED -
YOU CAN SPEAK TO THIS MOUNTAIN - MOVE! -
AND IT SHALL MOVE!
SO, BELOVED -
STAND TALL!
RAISE THE BANNER OF MY VICTORIOUS FAITH!
FOR YOUR WARRIOR KING -
THE LION OF THE TRIBE OF JUDAH IS A MIGHTY BAT-
TLE CRY -
IN THIS LAND FILLED WITH GIANTS!

(*Footnote)
Praise the Lord! Received this on Sept. 21, 1994

TEARS OF THE HEART

THERE ONCE WAS A BLIND MAN WHO CRIED OUT TO
THE CROWD:
"PLEASE TELL ME IF THE SUN IS WARM?"
"PLEASE TELL ME IF THE WIND IS BLOWING THROUGH
THE TREES!"
"PLEASE TELL ME WHAT COLOR ARE THE RAINDROPS!"

BUT THE CROWD WOULD WALK BY HIM.
NO ONE WOULD RESPOND OR GIVE ANSWER TO HIS
QUESTIONS.
SOME WOULD EVEN REMARK:
"THAT POOR MAN MUST HAVE LOST HIS MIND!"
SO EACH ONE WOULD NOT SEE OR HEAR OR EVEN
"SEE" THE POOR BLIND MAN!

TILL ONE DAY A CARPENTER'S SON WALKED BY AND
HE FIRST HEARD THE POOR MAN'S QUESTIONS TO THE
CROWD.
THE BLIND MAN HAD HEARD WONDROUS STORIES OF
A MAN WHO HEALED THE SICK -
HE ASKED WHO THIS MAN'S NAME WAS SO THAT HE
TOO CAN CALL OUT TO HIM AND BE HEALED.
SO AS THE CROWD CRIED OUT: "JESUS! JESUS!"
SO TOO HE CRIED OUT: "JESUS!"
ALL AROUND THE CARPENTER'S SON A THRONG OF
PEOPLE PRESSED AROUND HIM
ALL AROUND THE CARPENTER'S SON A CACOPHONY
OF VOICES BELLOWED IN HIS EARS -
YET -
HE HEARD A SOFT HEART CRY OUT: "JESUS!"

HE TURNED TO SEE WHOSE VOICE HE HEARD, AND HIS
EYES FELL UPON THE BLIND BEGGAR.
"WHAT WOULD YOU HAVE OF ME?" SPOKE THE QUIET
GENTLE CARPENTER'S SON.
"SIR! ARE YOU THE JESUS WHO THE CROWD IS SHOUT-
ING FOR ATTENTION?"
"I AM HE!"
THE BLIND MAN WAS PUZZLED FOR HE FELT A COOL
REFRESHING BREEZE DEEP WITHIN HIM -
SIR! ARE YOU THE JESUS OF WHOM I HAVE HEARD
ABOUT THAT HAS HEALED MANY PEOPLE?"
"I AM HE!"
AGAIN, THE BLIND MAN WAS PUZZLED FOR THIS TIME
HOPE FLUTTERED WITHIN HIS BOSOM!
"SIR! WOULD YOU RESTORE MY SIGHT SO THAT I MAY
SEE YOU?"
"YES!"
SUDDENLY!
HE SAW TREES WALKING BY HIM AND IN ASTONISH-
MENT HE REMARKED:
"I SEE TREES WALKING BY ME!"
"SIR! ARE PEOPLE REALLY JUST WALKING TREES?"
"IF THIS IS SEEING, I PREFER MY BLINDNESS!"
THEN QUIETLY, JESUS, TOUCHED HIS EYES -
AND LO!
THE   BLIND MAN'S EYES WERE OPENED!
THE   POOR BEGGAR LOOKED AROUND HIM -
THIS   TIME THERE WERE NO WALKING TREES -
THIS   TIME HE SAW WOUNDED SOLDIERS, TORMENT-
ING SLAVE DRIVERS -
HOT   TEARS FLOWED DOWN THE POOR BEGGAR,
FOR   NOW HE REALLY SAW WITH THE EYES OF HIS
HEART,
NOW HE KNEW THAT THE SON WAS WARM -
NOW HE KNEW THAT THERE WAS A CHANGING WIND
BLOWING IN THE "TREES"!"

NOW HE REALLY SEES JESUS, BUT NO CARPENTER'S
SON, WAS BEFORE HIM -
JESUS -
SON OF GOD!
AND IN HIS EYES HE SAW THE COLOR OF RAIN!
IN HIS EYES HE FELT THE WARMTH OF THE SUN!
IN HIS EYES HE KNEW HIS HEART'S CRY OF HOPE
WAS HEARD!
IN HIS EYES HE SAW HE WAS NOT A POOR BEG-
GAR -
BUT A SON OF THE MOST HIGH LORD!

NO WORDS OF GRATITUDE COULD HE SPEAK -
NO GESTURE OF THANKFULNESS COULD HE GIVE TO
HIS KING -
SO WITH HIS FINGER, HE GENTLY GATHERED A
TEARDROP FROM HIS OPENED EYES -
AND HE PRESENTED THIS SILVERY TEARDROP AS
THOUGH IT WERE A PRECIOUS PEARL -
AND JESUS THE "CARPENTER'S" SON TOOK THAT SIL-
VERY PEARL AND PLACED IT AMONG HIS MANY
OTHER PEARLS THAT WERE AROUND HIS NECK!

QUIETLY HE SUMMONED ME -
"COME!"
NOW AS HIS BELOVED SERVANT,
I HEAR THE MANY VOICES OF MY BROTHERS AND SIS-
TERS WHO ARE CRYING OUT: "JESUS! HEAL ME!"
NO GREATER WORLDLY TREASURE WOULD HE WANT
AS HIS REWARD -
ONLY A TEARDROP FROM THE HEART WOULD HE
RECEIVE!
SO -
"COME!"
LET US WALK WITH OUR MIGHTY KING!
LET US WORK WITH THE LORD OF THE HARVEST -

FOR THE HARVEST IS WHITE -
YES! BELOVED! THE COLOR OF RAIN IS WHITE!

(*Footnote)
Praise the Lord! Started this on 8/1/94 at 2:10 P.M. Finished this
"Masterpiece" from the Holy Spirit at 2:27 P.M. all Glory! All
honor be to my God! Hallelujah!

THE GREAT COMMISSION!

MARK 16

ARISE! ALL MY CHILDREN! ARISE!

ARISE! OH! MY BELOVED CHILDREN!
ARISE! ARISE FROM THY SLUMBER -
FOR THE DAWN OF YOUR SALVATION IS AT YOUR DOOR!
ARISE! MY BELOVED CHILDREN!
LOOK AROUND YOU, MY BELOVED CHILDREN -
DO YOU SEE THE SHADOWS OF DEATH TOUCHING MY OTHER CHILDREN WHO ARE LOST?
OH! MY BELOVED CHILDREN!
I NEED YOU TO GO OUT IN MY SON'S NAME AND AUTHORITY!
MY SON'S COMMISSION OF HEALING THE SICK, CASTING OUT DEMONS,
BEING AN AMBASSADOR OF RECONCILIATION -
GO FORTH AND RECONCILE WITH ONE ANOTHER IN MY AGAPE LOVE -
BE MENDED AND JOINED SO THAT MY GLORY CAN BLAZE THROUGH YOU -
LET US BE ONE IN MIND AND IN BODY -
SO THAT YOU CAN COME INTO MY PEACE AND REST!
SO NOW I GIVE YOU THIS COMMISSION -
"GO NOW, DESTROY THE PLANS OF OUR ENEMY TO BRING ALL LOST OUT OF THE DEN OF FOREVER TORMENT -
LET THE LIGHT OF MY SON'S LIFE BURN BRIGHTLY IN YOU -
BE BEACONS OF HOPE -
FOR NOW THE BLIND ARE SEARCHING FOR THE VISION OF TRUTH -
THE DEAF ARE STRAINING TO HEAR THE VOICE OF

LOVE -
THE HURT ARE CRYING FOR ARMS OF HEALING!

SO, MY BELOVED CHILDREN -
LET US GO TOGETHER AS ONE IN SPIRIT AND IN TRUTH -
LET US DRAW THE VICTIMS OF SATAN INTO THE KING-
DOM OF FREEDOM AND VICTORY!

(*Footnote)
Praise the Lord! Received this 5/31/93. Praise God!

WAKE-UP CALL TO THE CHURCH

ARISE, MY BELOVED CHILDREN!
ARISE, FROM YOUR DEEP SLUMBER!
DO YOU HEAR THE YOUNG LIONS ROARING?
DO YOU HEAR THE WOLVES TEARING AT THE WEAK?
ARISE, QUICKLY, MY BELOVED!
FOR THESE ARE PERILOUS TIMES!
YET -
BE NOT FAINT-HEARTED!
BE NOT FEARFUL!
LET MY LIFE BE YOUR LIFE -
LET MY WILL BE YOUR WILL -
LET MY HOLY SPIRIT GUIDE YOU THE WAY THROUGH
VICTORY!
FOR YES -
THE ENEMY IS GNASHING HIS TEETH!
HE ROAMS TO AND FRO IN THIS LAND -
HE GOES TO THE BYWAYS -
HE SEEKS THE WEAK -
HE SEEKS THE WOUNDED -
HE SEEKS THE INNOCENTS -
HE SEEKS THE LOST -
SO THAT HE MAY DESTROY THEM!
YET -
FEAR NOT!
CLING ONLY UNTO ME!
FOR I AM THE ROCK OF YOUR FAITH!
ANCHOR THYSELF FIRMLY AND DEEPLY IN ME -
FOR THESE ARE TRYING TIMES!
BE WARY MY BELOVED -

FOR THERE WILL BE THOSE WHO WILL SAY -
"HE IS THERE!"
"HE IS HERE!"
SEEK NOT THE VAIN AND FOOLISH WAYS OF THIS WORLD -
FOR THEY ARE THE PITFALLS OF YOUR DESTRUCTION!
LET NOT THE ENEMY ENSNARE YOU IN HIS NET OF DECEPTION!
BUT GATHER INTO THE ASSEMBLY OF THE ELDERS -
PRAISE AND WORSHIP ME -
DELIGHT THYSELVES IN ME -
IT IS NOT THAT I NEED THIS, BELOVED -
YET -
IT PLEASES ME TO SEE A HOLY NATION OF PRIESTS
SANCTIFIED AND SEPARATED UNTO ME!
FOR IF YOU DO NOT -
HOW CAN I BE IN THE MIDST OF THEE?
YES, BELOVED -
EVEN THE YOUNG MEN THAT WERE THROWN IN THE FIRE -
SANG PRAISES AND THEY WORSHIPPED THE LIVING GOD OF THEIR FOREFATHERS -
AND I WAS IN THE MIDST OF THEM!
AND MY GLORY SHONE GREATER THAN THE FIRE MAN CREATED -
AND HEARTS OF STONE, MELTED IN FEAR OF THE ONE TRUE LIVING GOD!
SO MY BELOVED -
ARISE!
DO NOT SLUMBER ANY LONGER!
I AM COMING!
SOON WE SHALL SEE EYE TO EYE!
WHAT EYE HAS NOT SEEN, WILL SEE CLEARLY!
WHAT EAR HAS NOT HEARD, WILL HEAR DISTINCTLY!
FOR I AM THE AUTHOR AND FINISHER OF THY FAITH!
I AM THE GOOD SHEPHERD!

MY FLOCK WILL ONLY HEED TO MY CALL!
THEY WILL NOT HEED NO STRANGER'S CALL!
BEWARE, BELOVED -
MANY WOLVES IN SHEEP'S CLOTHING ARE IN THE MIDST OF THEE!
BUT LET MY STAFF LEAD YOU TO GREEN PASTURES,
WHEN THE FLOODS OF DESPAIR WASH OVER YOU -
FEAR NOT!
FOR I WILL DELIVER YOU AND LEAD YOU TO STILL WATERS!
YES, BELOVED -
EVEN THOUGH YOU ARE WALKING IN THE VALLEY OF THE SHADOW OF DEATH -
FEAR NOT!
FOR I HAVE TAKEN DEATH'S STING AWAY!
SO COME!
LET US GATHER THE HARVEST -
FOR SOON -
THE FEAST WILL BE AWAITING YOU IN MY FATHER'S KINGDOM -
WE WILL GREET YOU IN OUR EVERLASTING GLORY!
A CROWN OF LIFE WILL BE YOUR REWARD FOR YOUR FAITHFULNESS!
YES, MY BELOVED CHILD,
YOU SHALL HEAR MY WORDS SPEAK INTO YOUR HEART -
"WELL DONE, MY GOOD AND FAITHFUL SERVANT!"
"COME AND SIT BY ME!"
"FOR NOW THERE IS NO MORE TEARS OR SORROW!"
"NOW IS EVERLASTING JOY AND PEACE!"
"COME!"
"ARISE!"
"SHINE BRIGHTLY IN THIS MIDNIGHT HOUR -
"THE DAWN OF YOUR HOPE IS ARISING -
"SO KISS THE SON AND GREET HIM AS A BLUSHING BRIDE WOULD GREET HER BRIDEGROOM -

"THE FEAST IS LAID OUT -
"THE GUESTS ARE COMING -
"THE ENEMY IS FOREVER VANQUISHED!"

(*Footnote)
Started this by the prompting and speaking of the Holy Spirit on 2/1/93 at 10:35 A.M and finished this at 10:50 A.M. Praise the Lord! For He is good and faithful! His Words are life unto my soul! Hallelujah! Hallelujah!

Amen!!!

IN THE SANDS OF TIME!

AS THE HOUR GLASS SLOWLY MEASURES THE PASS-
ING OF TIME -
SO, TOO, THY ENEMY MEASURES HIS TIME TO TOR-
MENT THEE!
YET -
FEAR NOT!
FOR AS THE HOUR GLASS CAN BE TURNED TO ONCE
AGAIN MEASURE THE PASSAGE OF TIME -
SO TOO, I MARK MY ADVERSARY'S TIME TO TEST THEE,
BELOVED!
YES!
THINK NOT THIS PASSAGE AS A TIME OF WEEPING AND
LAMENTING -
THINK NOT THESE ARE SORROWFUL PATHS OF TRIALS
AND TRIBULATIONS AS A STRANGE AND PECULIAR
WAY THAT I SHOW HOW MUCH I LOVE THEE -
RATHER, BELOVED SEE THAT I AM SEPARATING THEE
FROM THE CHAFF OF THE GOLDEN HARVEST!
SEE THAT I HAVE TURNED THE SANDS OF TIME
AGAINST MY ADVERSARY -
FOR HE SEEKS TO RULE AND REIGN -
FOR HE SEEKS TO BE "god" -
FOR HE SEEKS TO BE THY FATHER!

AS THE HOUR GLASS SLOWLY MEASURES THE PASS-
ING OF TIME -
SO TOO, BELOVED -
I MEASURE THY PASSAGE THROUGH THIS LIFE!
FOR AS MY CHILDREN OF THE LIGHT -
YOU WILL REJOICE WHEN THE CHILDREN OF THE

DARKNESS -
MOCK AND SCORN YOU -
PERSECUTE AND REJECT YOU!
FOR AS MY ONLY BEGOTTEN SON WAS REJECTED BY
THE CHILDREN OF ISRAEL -
MY FIRST CHOSEN -
SO TOO, I HAVE GATHERED ANOTHER SHEEPFOLD!
FOR MY SON WALKED UPON THY SHORES AND WIT-
NESSED A WILD FLOCK WITH NO SHEPHERD TO LEAD
AND GUIDE THEM -
YES, BELOVED, YOU ARE OF THAT SHEEPFOLD -
AS THE UNBELIEVERS CAME TO MY SON -
BEGGING FOR THE CRUMBS OF LIFE -
SO TOO, BELOVED -
I SNATCHED THEE AWAY FROM THE JAWS OF DEATH!

SO COME!
WALK IN THE VICTORY OF CALVARY!
WALK ABOVE THE SANDS OF TIME -
NOT BE OVERCOME AND SMOTHERED BY THE GRAINS
OF STRIFE, HATRED AND BITTERNESS!
FOR AS YOU COME CLOSER TO ME -
I WILL BE DRAWN CLOSER TO THEE!
AS YOU RAISE UP SONGS OF PRAISE TO ME -
I SHALL RAISE THEE ABOVE OUR ENEMIES!
SO BE NOT FAINT-HEARTED WHEN THE STORM BLOWS -
AND THE SANDS OF TIME WHIP AT YOU IN THE FURY
OF OUR ENEMIES HATRED
BUT STAND FIRM!
BE STILL!
SEE THY FATHER VANQUISH THY ENEMIES!
YES, BELOVED AS YOU BLESS AND FORGIVE THY
ENEMIES -
YOU WILL BE PUTTING HOT COALS OF MY WRATH
UPON THEIR HEADS!
YET -

REJOICE NOT AT SUCH VICTORIES -
RATHER, BELOVED -
PRAY WITH MY HOLY SPIRIT INCESSANTLY!
FOR WHO IN THE SHIFTING PASSAGE OF TIME WILL
INTERCEDE FOR THE NATIONS?
FOR WHO IN THIS SHIFTING PASSAGE OF TIME WILL
INTERCEDE FOR THE TRIBE OF JUDAH?
FOR WHO IN THIS SHIFTING PASSAGE OF TIME WILL
INTERCEDE FOR THE CITY OF JERUSALEM?
MY PRECIOUS BELOVED CHILD -
YOU ARE THE GRAINS OF MY LOVE -
YOU ARE THE GRAINS OF HOPE IN THESE DARK PASS-
ING MOMENTS -
SO STAND FIRM IN THE MIDST OF THE WHIRLWIND -
SEE THE GLORY OF THY FATHER IN THE HOURGLASS
OF THY SALVATION!
FOR WITHIN THEE ARE THE PRECIOUS DROPS OF
ATONEMENT SHED BY MY ONLY BEGOTTEN SON ON A
CURSED TREE UPON A HILL CALLED -
GOLGOTHA!

YET, BELOVED, AS THE SANDS ON A SURF-BEATEN
SHORE ABSORB THESE PRECIOUS DROPS OF LIFE DEEP
WITHIN THEE -
FOR AS THE ENEMY COMES UPON THEE AS AN ANGRY
SWELL BEATS UPON THY SHORE -
SEE THY ANCHOR -
SEE THY BUTTRESS THAT CALMS THE WAYWARD CUR-
RENTS THAT WOULD SWEEP THEE AWAY FROM ME!
YET -
BELOVED -
HEAR MY WORDS OF COVENANT WITH THEE -
NOTHING CAN EVER SEPARATE ME FROM THEE
EXCEPT THY UNBELIEF!
I'VE PLACED MY BOW IN THE HEAVENLIES FOR THY
SECURE HOPE -

ALL IS WELL, MY BELOVED!
FOR I SEE THE SONGLOW DEEP WITHIN THEE!
SO COME!
WALK ABOVE THE GRAINS OF TIME -
WALK UPON THE SHORES OF MY EVERLASTING LIFE!
SEE NOT THE HOURGLASS AS THE PLACE OF BONDAGE -
BUT DIVE DEEPLY WITHIN THE GRAINS OF TIME -
IN MY SON'S NAME, BRING OUT THE CAPTIVES, HEAL
THE WOUNDED, LET THE LIGHT OF MY WORD BE A
GUIDE INTO MY KINGDOM FOR THOSE WHO HAVE
LOST THEIR WAY HOME!

(*Footnote)
Started this on 8/30/94 at 8:10 A.M. Finished this at 8:40 A.M.
Praise and glory to my God!

HEAR THE CALL, TAKE A STAND!

EVERYONE MARCHES TO A DIFFERENT DRUM-BEAT -
EVERYONE WALKS THEIR PATHS OF DESTINY -
BUT DOES ANYONE HEAR THE CALL OF THE LORD?
AS WE GO ABOUT OUR DAILY ROUTINE -
DO WE STILL OUR INNER VOICE TO HEAR THE CALL OF
THE LORD?

AS WE HURRY IN OUR LIVES, IN THIS AGE OF CONFU-
SION AND CHAOS -
DO WE STILL OUR LOUD DEMANDING INNER VOICE?
DO WE STILL OUR HUMAN NATURE?

BE STILL PEOPLE!
HEAR THE CALL OF THE LORD!
HE IS DEEP WITHIN US - IN OUR SECRET TEMPLE!
DO YOU HEAR HIS QUIET PLEA?
HE IS CALLING YOU TO EMBRACE HIS GREATER LOVE
FOR US!
HE IS CALLING YOU TO EMBRACE HIS POOR AND
NEEDY CHILDREN!
THE LORD SAITH:
"LOVE MY CHILDREN, AS I LOVE YOU!"
"TAKE A STAND WITH ME - NOT AGAINST ME!"
"FOR IF YOU REJECT ME -
"YOUR LIFE IS MEANINGLESS AND LOVELESS!"
"THEN YOU ARE THE CHILDREN OF MY ENEMY -
"YOUR FATHER OF DARKNESS THAT COMES AS A
ROARING LION TO KILL AND DESTROY MY SHEEP!"

OH! SAINTS OF THE MOST HIGH GOD OF ISRAEL FALL
ON YOUR KNEES -
CRY FOR THE LOST -
INTERCEDE FOR THE BACKSLIDER -
TRAVAIL FORTH THE NEWBORN BABES OF THE SPIRIT -
LABOR IN THE GOLDEN FIELDS OF THE LORD -
FOR GREAT AND WHITE IS THE HARVEST -
SOON THE REAPERS WILL BE SENT FORTH TO GATHER
THE HARVEST -
WILL YOU BE THE GRAIN OF LIFE -
OR WILL YOU BE THE THISTLE - THE TARES THAT
TRIED TO STEAL THE WHEAT'S LIFE AS IT GREW?

OH! NATIONS, TRIBES OF THIS WORLD -
HEAR THE MIGHTY ROAR OF THE LION OF THE TRIBE
OF JUDAH -
TREMBLE ALL YE MOUNTAINS -
YOUR MAJESTIC LORD AND KING IS COMING FOR HIS
WONDROUS BRIDE!
BRIDE OF CHRIST - HEAR THE CALL OF YOUR BRIDE-
GROOM - TAKE A STAND BY HIS SIDE!

PROPHECY 9/13/92

COME, MY BELOVED!
COME, AND HEAR THE SHOUTS OF VICTORY!
YES, NIGHT IS APPROACHING -
BUT, SEE THE BRIGHT MORNING STAR -
WITH EVERY NIGHT-FALL THERE IS A PROMISE OF A
BRIGHT NEW DAWN!
YES, MY BELOVED -
NIGHT KEEPS YOU BLINDED -
BUT LET MY LOVE ENTER THEE -
AND YOU SHALL SEE THE GLORY OF MY KINGDOM!
THIS IS YOUR INHERITANCE, MY BELOVED!
SO FEAR NOT!
COME, GATHER ROUND ME -
FOR AS YOU COME AS ONE IN BODY, MIND AND IN
SPIRIT -
AS YOU INTERCEDE WITH ME FOR THOSE WHO ARE
LOST IN THE DARKNESS -
I WILL BE IN THE MIDST OF THEE AND MY PRESENCE
WILL DRAW THE LOST -
THE WOUNDED, THE BLINDED BY THE BATTLE THAT IS
IN THIS LAND!
BUT, REMEMBER, BELOVED -
GREATER THINGS WILL YOU DO IN MY NAME -
SO STAND BOLDLY IN THE AUTHORITY I HAVE GIVEN
YOU!
GO NOW, PROCLAIM THE KING IS RETURNING!
WALK WITH ME IN VICTORY!
FOR CALVARY IS YOUR STANDARD -
AND MY BLOOD CLEANSES AND HEALS ALL THAT WAS
INFLICTED UPON YOU BY OUR ENEMIES!

SO, COME!
THE LION OF THE TRIBE OF JUDAH IS ROARING WITH
VICTORY IN THIS LAND!

MIGHTY WARRIOR
BY JESUS, COMMANDER AND KING!

HO! MIGHTY WARRIOR!
WHERE ART THOU GOING?
HO! MIGHTY WARRIOR!
THOU ART FULLY DRESSED IN WAR GARMENTS -
ART THOU NOW IN BATTLE?
WHO IS YOUR ENEMY?
FOR I SEE NO BATTLEGROUND -
FOR I SEE NO ENEMIES ROUND ABOUT YOUR CAMP!

WELL!
SIRE! AND WHOM MIGHT THOU BE?
THOU ART IN GARMENTS OF A SERVANT -
DID THOU COMEST TO DO SERVICE UP TO ME?
THOU SEEST NOT MY ENEMY -
YET -
FOR I SEE THE BATTLEGROUND ROUND ABOUT US!
FOR I SEE MY ENEMIES ROUND ABOUT US!
SEE!
THERE!
HOW MY ENEMIES LURK IN THE SHADOWS!
COME! WE MUST WAGE A GRAND BATTLE!

HO! MIGHTY WARRIOR!
WHERE IS YOUR COMMANDER?
DO YOU TAKE UPON THYSELF TO WAGE BATTLE
AGAINST UNSEEN ENEMIES?
DO YOU NOT RECOGNIZE WHO I AM?
YOU SEE THE BATTLE -

YOU SEE THE ENEMY -
YET -
DO YOU NOT SEE YOUR COMMANDER?
THOU ART A MIGHTY WARRIOR -
BUT WHERE IS YOUR STANDARD?
THOU ART A MIGHTY WARRIOR -
BUT WHO IS YOUR LIEGE LORD?
MIGHTY WARRIOR YOU HAVE WEAPONS FASHIONED
TO DO BATTLE WITH ENEMIES OF FLESH AND BONE -
YET -
YOU SPEAK OF YOUR ENEMY AS SHADOWS!
CAN YOU HAVE VICTORY AS YOU STAND HERE BEFORE
ME IN YOUR FINERY OF WAR?

SIRE!
WHO ART THOU?
THOU SPEAKEST IN SUCH STRANGE WAYS,
YOU COME TO ME IN SERVANT GARMENT,
YET -
YOU HAVE A CARRIAGE OF AUTHORITY ROUND ABOUT
THEE!
DO YOU MOCK ME, SIRE?
I HAVE NO NEED FOR A COMMANDER!
FOR I AM THE COMMANDER!
I HAVE THE AUTHORITY TO WAGE WAR WITH MY
ENEMY!
BUT... YET -
THOU SEEST NOT MY ENEMY!
WHAT MATTER OF MAN ART THOU?
I HAVE NO NEED TO BEAR ANYONE'S STANDARD!
FOR I BEAR MY OWN UNTO BATTLE!
MY WEAPONS MAY SEEM FOOLISH TO THEE!
YET -
THERE ARE NO WEAPONS FASHIONED FOR SUCH AN
ELUSIVE FOE!
YES -

VICTORY ELUDES ME!
JUST AS MY ENEMIES ATTACK UPON ME!
FOR I BECOME WOUNDED -
YET -
NO WEAPON WAS WEALED UPON ME!
HAS THOU ANY KNOWLEDGE TO COME BEFORE ME
AND REBUKE ME FOR DOING BATTLE IN MY OWN WIS-
DOM?

HO! MIGHTY WARRIOR!
DRESSED IN MIGHTY GARMENTS OF WAR!
CAST ASIDE THESE GARMENTS!
CAST ASIDE YOUR FINE WEAPONS!
CAST ASIDE YOUR GRAND WISDOM!
CAST ASIDE YOUR AUTHORITY!
COME TO ME MIGHTY WARRIOR!
BEAR MY STANDARD IN YOUR BATTLE!
BUT! KNOW THIS, MIGHTY WARRIOR, THE BATTLE
BELONGS TO THE LORD!
YOUR BATTLE IS ON YOUR KNEES, INTERCEDING FOR
THE VICTORY OF MY LOST CHILDREN!
YOUR BATTLE IS TO STAND FIRMLY ON THE VICTORY I
WON WITH MY SHED BLOOD ON CALVARY!
FOR YOUR ENEMIES ARE MY ENEMIES, TOGETHER AS
ONE, MY FATHER'S GLORY WILL SHINE FORTH IN THIS
LAND FILLED WITH GIANTS!

HO! MIGHTY WARRIOR!
DRESS IN THESE BATTLE GARMENTS I COMMISSION
THEE TO WEAR DAILY!
PUT ON YOUR HELMET OF SALVATION -
AS I BECOME YOUR LORD -
I SHALL BECOME YOUR SAVIOR AND DELIVERER IN
TIMES OF GREAT TRIBULATION!
GIRD YOUR LOINS, MIGHTY WARRIOR, WITH THE BELT
OF TRUTH -

LET MY TRUTH GIRD YOUR SOUL WITH WORDS OF LIFE AND VICTORY!

PUT ON THE BREASTPLATE OF RIGHTEOUSNESS -

THE ENEMY WILL SEE YOUR WEAKNESSES, MIGHTY WARRIOR -

BUT AS YOU BELIEVE IN ME -

THAT MY WORDS -

"GREATER THINGS YOU SHALL DO IN MY NAME -"

YOUR SOUL WILL NOT BE INFLICTED BY THE MANY FIERY DARTS OF THE ENEMY.

FOR AS THE FATHER SENT ME TO DELIVER OUR CHIL-DREN,

TO SET THE CAPTIVES FREE -

SO TOO I GIVE YOU THE SAME COMMISSION -

IN MY NAME -

CAST OUT THE ENEMY -

HEAL THE SICK AND THE WOUNDED -

RAISE THE DEAD!

MIGHTY WARRIOR, SHOD THY FEET WITH MY GOOD NEWS TO THE PEOPLE OF THIS LAND!

FOR UNTO ME, YOU SHALL BE MIGHTY WITNESSES,

WITH THE HELPER WHO WILL EMPOWER YOU -

SO THAT MY FATHER'S GLORY WILL SHINE FORTH AS A BEACON OF HOPE TO THE LOST!

MIGHTY WARRIOR, TAKE THY SHIELD OF FAITH, FOR AS THE ENEMY WIELDS HIS WEAPONS UPON YOU THEY SHALL HAVE NO POWER TO INFLICT YOU,

FOR UPON THIS SHIELD MY STANDARD WILL BE EMBLAZONED UPON IT -

FOR NO WEAPONS FASHIONED AGAINST THEE SHALL PREVAIL!

MIGHTY WARRIOR!

TAKE THIS SWORD WHICH IS OF MY HOLY SPIRIT WHICH SPEAKETH FORTH FROM THY LIPS MY FATHER'S WORDS OF VICTORY!

SEE HOW THIS MIGHTY SWORD PIERCES THE ENEMY'S HEART!
FOR HE SHALL FLEE FROM THEE!

SO, COME, MIGHTY WARRIOR -
LET US BATTLE THE ENEMY -
LET US SET FREE THE CAPTIVES -
LET US GUIDE THE LOST SOULS TO THEIR RIGHTFUL PLACE -
IN MY FATHER'S KINGDOM, WHERE THEY ARE CO-HEIRS WITH ME!
LET US HEAL THE WOUNDED AND AFFLICTED, SO PRAISES WILL RISE UP TO MY FATHER'S THRONE AND HE SHALL FIND THE SWEET FRAGRANCE OF THY SACRIFICE HOLY AND PLEASING!

HO! MIGHTY WARRIOR!
COME!
FOLLOW ME!
AS YOUR LORD AND KING -
I SHALL NEVER DEPART FROM THEE!
NO TRIBULATIONS -
NO SINS THAT HAVE BEEN WASHED WITH MY HOLY BLOOD, AND BY THE WASHING OF MY FATHER'S WORDS -
WILL KEEP ME AWAY FROM THEE!
FOR MY LOVE IS GREAT!
SEE, NO MAN HAS GREATER LOVE THAN THAT ONE SHOULD LAY DOWN HIS LIFE FOR ANOTHER -
BELOVED -
I HAVE WILLINGLY LAID DOWN MY LIFE -
SO THAT YOU WILL HAVE EVERLASTING LIFE!
COME, BELOVED,
REST NOW WITH ME, LET ME REFRESH AND RENEW YOU THIS MOMENT -
FOR GREAT IS THE STORM OF DARKNESS AND DESPAIR

THAT IS COMING UPON YOU -
YET - FEAR NOT!
REMEMBER -
NEVER WILL I FORSAKE YOU, MY BELOVED, MY
BRIDE!
WEAR MY CROWN OF GLORY UPON THEE,
PUT ON THE GARMENT OF FINE LINEN,
PUT ON THE GARMENT OF PRAISE,
FOR I, YOUR BRIDEGROOM, AM RETURNING VERY SOON!
LABOR FOR A MOMENT LONGER, BELOVED -
BUT SEE, AS THE NIGHT FALLETH -
DAWN IS A SWEET HOPE -
FOR I AM THE BRIGHT MORNING STAR -
AND YE ARE MY STARS OF GLORY!

(*Footnote)
Praise the Lord! First received this on 2/17/90, added on 6/24/94.
Praise the Lord! Forever and ever! Amen!

OF BLESSINGS AND CURSES...

GARDEN OF TEARS

IN A TIME LONG AGO -
WHEN A SOLITARY LIFE WALKED UPON THE SANDS OF
HUMANITY HE WENT TO A GARDEN -
THIS GARDEN'S NAME WAS GETHSEMANE -
WITH A HEART SO HEAVY -
SILENT TEARS FELL FROM HIS SOUL-WORN IMAGE!
UPON A ROCK FOR SUPPORT TO HIS TREMBLING BODY -
HE FELL UPON HIS KNEES -
HE LAID HIS HEAD UPON THE STONE -
IN ANGUISH HE POURED HIS TEARS UPON THIS ROCK -
SO GRIEF-STRICKEN WAS THIS MAN OF SORROWS!
WHY WAS HE ALONE?
WHY COULDN'T HIS FRIENDS SEE HIS ANGUISH AND
COMFORT HIM?

HERE I SIT IN A GARDEN -
THIS GARDEN'S NAME IS BRANCH BROOK PARK YET -
IT JUST AS WELL BE CALLED GETHSEMANE!
THOUGH THERE IS NO ROCK HERE IN THIS PLACE -
YET -
IN MY HEART A SOLITARY MOUNTAIN'S PEAK REACH-
ES FOR THE HEAVENS!
THIS MOUNTAIN'S NAME IS JESUS OF NAZARETH!

TEARS STREAM DOWN MY AGE WORN FACE.
HERE, TOO, I AM ALL ALONE -
NO ONE TO SEE MY TEARS -
NO ONE TO HEAR MY SOBS OF ANGUISH -
NO ONE TO COMFORT MY TORN HEART -
NO ONE TO HEAL MY WOUNDED SPIRIT -

NO ONE TO SPEAK TO MY SOUL -
                    "ALL IS WELL!"

THE WIND BLEW A SINGLE DRY GOLDEN LEAF
THROUGH MY WINDOW -
I TOSSED IT OUT!
IT JOINED SO MANY MULTI-HUED FALLEN LEAVES -
AS I WATCHED -
A GENTLE WIND WOULD STIR THEM AROUND -
SOME WOULD BE LIFTED -
BUT SOON FELL TO THE GROUND.
AS A CAR WOULD RACE BY -
IN THE WAKE OF THAT MOTION -
A FEW LEAVES WOULD TRAVEL AFTER IT -
SUDDENLY!
IN THE STRONG RUSTLE OF THE WIND -
I HEAR A VOICE -
"CHILD, WHY ARE YOU SO DOWNCAST?"
"CHILD, COME OUT OF THE VALLEY OF DESPAIR" -

AS I WATCH -
A LEAF BECAME AIRBORNE!
THE WIND SUSTAINED ITS FLIGHT UPWARD!
IT WAS AS THOUGH THE LEAF WENT BACK TO WHERE
IT BELONGED!
AS I WATCHED THAT GOLDEN-RUSSET SOLITARY LEAF
SWIRL UPWARD IN THE BREEZE THAT CAUGHT IT -
I FELT MY SOUL ALSO BE CAUGHT UP AND MY BAT-
TLE-SCARRED WOUNDED SPIRIT ROSE UP ALSO!
UPWARD WE WENT!
THE VALLEY BELOW -
THE WIND GENTLE YET FIRMLY LIFTED US UP!
SOON WE DRIFTED DOWNWARD -
WE LANDED ON A MOUNTAINTOP GARDEN!
GLISTENING INTRICATELY CARVED WHITE BENCHES
NESTLED BELOW A TREE

OF MANY DIFFERENT FRUITS UPON ITS BRANCHES -
HOW CAN THIS BE?
UPON A GOLDEN PATH -
A STRANGER WALKED TOWARDS ME -
ARMS OUTSTRETCHED IN A WARM, HEARTY WELCOME -
AS THOUGH I WAS LONG GONE AND NOW RETURNED
HOME!
AS THIS MAN CAME CLOSER -
HIS HEAD WAS COVERED WITH A LINEN CLOTH -
SLIGHTLY HIDING HIS FACE -
HIS OVERCOAT OF MANY HUES -
WIDE OPEN IN THE GENTLE WARM BREEZE -
HIS UNDER GARMENT OF PURE WHITE LINEN -
HIS HEM APPEARED BLOODSTAINED -
HIS FEET SHOD IN GOLDEN BEJEWELED SANDALS -
UPON HIS BREAST -
THERE WAS A GOLDEN COLLAR HOLDING TWELVE DIF-
FERENT COLORED JEWELS IN A HOUSE LIKE DESIGN.

I KNOW THIS MAN!
SUDDENLY!
I KNEW HIM!
HE'S MY ADONAI!
HE'S THE LORD OF THIS MOUNTAINTOP GARDEN!
I RAN INTO HIS OPEN ARMS -
RESTED MY HEAD UPON HIS MUSCULAR SHOULDER -
HE WRAPPED HIS STRONG, GENTLE ARMS AROUND ME!
JUST LIKE A FATHER WOULD HOLD HIS HURTING
CHILD!
TEARS RAN DOWN -
SOBS MUFFLED IN HIS CHEST -
HIS HAND CARESSING MY FEVERED HEAD -
AND I FELT HIS CALM SOOTHING LOVE UPON ME!

IT WAS LIKE A HEALING SALVE TO MY OPEN WOUNDS -
THE ENEMY HAD INFLICTED UPON ME!

NO PASSAGE OF TIME WAS FELT OR SEEN -
SLOWLY PEACE FLOWED FROM HIM INTO MY SOUL
INTO MY SPIRIT!
WHAT WAS TORN ASUNDER -
HE HEALED AND MADE WHOLE!
SLOWLY, I LIFTED MY HEAD AND I GAZED INTO HIS
FACE -
SUCH LOVE IN THOSE BLUE-GREEN EYES!
YET -
HE TOO, HAD CRIED HIS TEARS UPON MY HEAD!
SOFTLY, HE SPOKE TO ME -
"BELOVED! KNOW YOU NOT THAT MY EYE IS UPON
THE SPARROW?"
"BELOVED! KNOW YOU NOT TO CAST MY CROSS UPON
THE BITTER WATERS -
"THAT I WILL MAKE IT SWEET?"
"BELOVED! KNOW YOU NOT THAT THOUGH THE
FLOOD-GATES HAVE OPENED AND THE WAVES ARE
BILLOWING UPON THEE -
"YET -
"THEY SHALL NOT OVERTAKE THEE?"
MY HEAD LOWERED,
MY HEART KNEW HIS WORDS WERE TRUE -
HOW DID I ALLOW MYSELF TO BE UNGUARDED TO
THE ENEMY'S BLOW?

"COME! MY PRECIOUS CHILD!"
"COME AND REST WITH US FOR A WHILE!"
"I SHALL MAKE YOU AS A WELL WATERED GARDEN
"FOR I AM THY HUSBANDMAN!"
IN MY HEART, MY FATHER'S WORDS AT FIRST DRIZ-
ZLED INTO MY PARCHED SPIRIT -
THEN, THIRSTILY I DRANK TO QUENCH MY BURNING
THROAT!"

"PRECIOUS!"
"HERE IS THY GARMENT OF BATTLE -"
"YET -"
"WEAR MY MANTLE OF JOY ROUND ABOUT THEE -"
"FOR THIS IS YOUR STRENGTH IN THE TIMES OF HARD BATTLE!" "LET MY WORDS BE YOUR WORDS OF MERCY AND COMPASSION TO THOSE WHO HAVE FALLEN TO THE ENEMY'S BLOW OF DEATH!"

THERE IN MY ABBA FATHER'S GARDEN CALLED LOVE -
I WAS COMFORTED -
> HEALED -
> STRENGTHENED -
> WELL-RESTED!

"NOW, MY PRECIOUS BELOVED -"
MY ADONAI SPOKE LOVINGLY TO ME -
"IT IS TIME TO RETURN TO THE VALLEY OF DESPAIR -"
"YET -"
"IN YOUR HEART, KEEP THIS GARDEN OF LOVE IN YOUR REMEMBRANCE -
"FOR AS I SEND YOU TO THE WOUNDED CHILDREN -"
"I WILL HEAL THEM IF THEY WILL ACKNOWLEDGE ME AND DENOUNCE ALLEGIANCE WITH OUR ENEMIES -"
"I WILL COMFORT THEM IF THEY SURRENDER THEIR MOURNING -"
"I WILL PUT MY WORDS AS MANNA TO THOSE THAT ARE HUNGRY FOR RIGHTEOUSNESS!"
"I WILL CALL UNTO ME THE PEACE-MAKERS HERE UPON MY MOUNT -"
"I SHALL SEND THEM AS A MIGHTY COMPANY -"
"TO SOUND MY TRUMPET OF RETURN!"
"FOR THE WATCHMEN UPON THE TOWERS TO RESOUND THE VICTORY CALL!"
"THE MASTER OF THE HOUSE HAS RETURNED!"
"LET HIS BRIDE COME TO GREET HER BRIDEGROOM!"
"FOR THE ENEMY IS FOREVER VANQUISHED!"

(*Footnote)

I started this on 10/28/00 at 12:00 P.M. - Finished this at 1:00 P.M. Thank you Abba Father! Thank you my precious Adonai - Jesus of Nazareth! Thank you my Holy Spirit for bringing me home for a rest and healing! Praise and glory and honor be forever to my God! Hallelujah!

LABOR OF LOVE!

ONCE THERE WAS A CARPENTER'S SON -
WITH HIS HAMMER -
WITH HIS SAW -
WITH HIS GIMLET -
WITH HIS SCREWS -
WITH HIS PLANE -
WITH HIS RULER -
WITH HIS SANDPAPER -
HE CAME INTO HIS WORKSHOP, HE PUT ON HIS APRON -
HIS PURPOSE TO MAKE A PULPIT!

THE CARPENTER'S SON REACHED OUT TO SELECT HIS
GIMLET -
GENTLY WITH THIS TOOL, HE BEGAN TO IMPRESS THE
DESIGN OF HIS WILL UPON THE BLANK COARSE
WOOD, BUT AS SOON AS HE STARTED TO WORK THE
WOOD,
IT BEGAN TO SPLINTER AND CRACK!
AND THE WOOD'S NATURAL GRAIN CREATED IT'S OWN
DESIGNS!
THE CARPENTER'S SON COULDN'T CONTINUE HIS
WORK PLANS -
HE HAD TO FIRST SMOOTH AWAY THESE IMPERFEC-
TIONS -
HOW CAN HE?
THIS PARTICULAR KIND OF WOOD CAME FROM A TREE
THAT LIVED IN THE DESERT!
SO WORKING WITH IT WAS A DIFFICULT, TEDIOUS
LABOR!
ONCE AGAIN, THE CARPENTER REACHED OUT FOR A

TOOL -
THIS TIME HE SELECTED A RULER -
WITH THE RULER HE MEASURED THE LENGTH, THE
WIDTH, AND THE DEPTH OF THE WOOD.
THEN HE SELECTED A PENCIL, WITH IT HE MARKED
HIS WILL AND HIS PURPOSE!

ONCE AGAIN, THE CARPENTER'S SON BEGAN HIS
LABOR OF LOVE!
THIS TIME HE REACHED OUT AND SELECTED A PLANE
TOOL.
AS HE CAREFULLY GLIDED THE CUTTING EDGE OF THE
PLANE ACROSS, HE SLOUGHED OFF THE IMPERFEC-
TIONS, DEEPER INTO THE WOOD HE WENT TIL HE
REACHED THE PERFECT SURFACE DEPTH!
OVER AND OVER WOULD THE CARPENTER'S SON USE
THE GIMLET, THE PLANE,
THE RULER AND THE PENCIL -
LAYER BY LAYER -
DEEPER INTO THE WOOD -
WOULD HE SEARCH -
TILL AT LAST -
THERE WAS NO MORE CRACKING OR SPLINTERING!
AT LAST -
THE FIRST IMPRESSION OF HIS PULPIT BECAME
CLEAR!

IN DELIGHT, THE CARPENTER'S SON REACHED OUT
AND SELECTED HIS SAW -
WITH CAREFUL DELIBERATE PRECISION -
HE WOULD CUT OFF THE UNWANTED PIECES OF WOOD
THAT WERE NOT IN HIS PLANS,
TO WHICH HE HAD LABORED SO LONG TO ACHIEVE!
HERE AT LAST -

STANDING BEFORE HIM WAS A ROUGH HEWN WOODEN PULPIT!

NOW, THE CARPENTER'S SON NEEDED TO CREATE HIS OWN UNIQUE DESIGNS WITHIN THE WOOD.

WITH A BLUE-PRINT OF HIS TASK SET BEFORE HIM - HE BEGAN WITH JOY TO FASHION HIS PULPIT!

ONCE AGAIN, HE REACHED OUT FOR HIS TOOLS - THIS TIME HE SELECTED THE SANDPAPER.

AS HE RUBBED AWAY THE ROUGHNESS - THE WOOD BEGAN TO SHINE WITH AN INNER GLOW!

IT'S NATURAL BEAUTY ROSE UP AS THE SANDPAPER SMOOTHED OUT THE ROUGHNESS!

"YES!"

EXCLAIMED THE CARPENTER'S SON IN DELIGHT!

"ALL WILL SEE THIS WONDROUS LABOR I HAVE DONE!"

"YOU, MY BELOVED PULPIT, I WILL USE FOR MY FATHER'S GLORY!

"SO ALL CAN SEE AND DESIRE TO BE AS YOU!"

WITH GLADNESS IN HIS HEART -

WITH SONGS OF JOY, HE PRESSED ON WITH HIS LABOR OF LOVE!

THIS TIME THE CARPENTER'S SON REACHED OUT AND SELECTED HIS HAMMER,

HIS NAILS AND SCREWS.

NOW, HE PICKED UP THE VARIOUS PIECES OF WOOD HE HAD PERFECTED TO HIS DESIGN -

CAREFULLY HE MATCHED UP EACH PIECE TO ONE ANOTHER -

AS THEY FITTED PERFECTLY -

HE HAMMERED HIS NAILS INTO THE WOOD-PIECES - SO EXPERTLY DID HE JOIN THEM -

YOU COULD NOT SEE THE JOINING SEAMS!

NOW HE CAME TO THE MOST DIFFICULT TASK!

THIS PULPIT NEEDED A DOOR -

FOR HOW CAN HE STAND BEHIND IT -

IF NO ONE CAN SEE OR HEAR HIM!
SO WITH SCREWS AND HINGES, HAMMER AND RULER,
AND SANDPAPER AND PLANE AND GIMLET HE FASH-
IONED HIS DOOR!
THEN HE ALIGNED THE DOOR ACCORDING TO HIS
PLANS AND DESIGN AND ATTACHED HIS DOOR!

THE CARPENTER'S SON PRESENTED HIS GIFT TO HIS
FATHER -
WITH DELIGHT AND JOY, HIS FATHER RECEIVED HIS
SON'S LABOR OF LOVE HE PRAISED HIM AND GAVE
HIM HONOR AND PRIVILEGES OF A MASTER CARPEN-
TER!
FOR NOW THEY HAD A PULPIT WHERE THEY COULD
TELL HIS CHILDREN -
TELL HIS NEIGHBORS -
TELL HIS CITY -
"I AM YOUR KING -"
"COME INTO MY HOUSE -"
"THERE'S A WEDDING TO ATTEND!"
"MY SON HAS FOUND HIMSELF A BEAUTIFUL, MAGNIF-
ICENT BRIDE!
"COME AND SEE HER BEAUTY!"
"COME TO THE WEDDING FEAST!"
"COME!"

MY BELOVED,
YOU ARE MY PULPIT -
IN TENDER PATIENT LOVE I HAVE FASHIONED THEE -
MY PRECIOUS LITTLE ONE -
YOU ARE MY DOOR FOR ALL TO SEE THE BRIDEGROOM
WITHIN THEE!
WILL THOU KEEPEST THY DOOR OPEN -
OR WILL THOU KEEPEST SHUT TIGHT?

YES -
BELOVED -
YOU ARE ALSO THE BRIDE OF MY ONLY BEGOTTEN SON -
IN LOVE I HAVE FASHIONED THEE -
IN LOVE I WILL JOIN THEE AS ONE -
WILL YOU ACCEPT HIS LIFE AS YOURS?
WILL YOU LET YOUR KING SPEAK THROUGH YOU TO
ALL OF HIS LOST CHILDREN?
WILL YOU ALLOW THE WOUNDED SOLDIERS -
THE SEEKING HEART TO COME INTO MY HOUSE TO BE
HEALED AND CARED FOR?
I HAVE FASHIONED THEE, MY BELOVED -
I HAVE CREATED YOU IN MY IMAGE -
I HAVE GIVEN YOU MY ONLY BEGOTTEN SON -
WITH MY BREATH OF LIFE, I HAVE KISSED YOU,
BELOVED -
WILL THOU BE MINE?
WILL THOU ALSO LABOR WITH ME?
FOR IF YOU ARE TRULY MINE -
THE ENEMY CANNOT COME BETWEEN US!
HE CANNOT HARM OR DESTROY YOU ANY MORE, MY
BELOVED!
THIS IS THE GIFT I GIVE YOU -
THE FREEDOM TO CHOOSE -
AS MY BRIDE -
I WILL GIVE THEE EVERLASTING ABUNDANT LIFE,
A CROWN OF GLORY I WILL PLACE UPON THY HEAD,
IN PURE WHITE LINEN I WILL CLOTHE THEE,
WITH A CRIMSON OVERCOAT TO SHOW ALL
FROM WHOSE HOUSEHOLD YOU COME FROM!
SEE MY PRECIOUS LITTLE ONES -
HOW TRULY WONDERFUL IS THE "CARPENTER'S"
LABOR OF LOVE IS!

DO YOU HEAR YOUR KING KNOCKING AT THE DOOR OF YOUR HEART?

WILL YOU BE LIKE THE INNKEEPER SAYING:
"THERE'S NO MORE ROOM HERE! GO SOMEWHERE ELSE!"
FOR THE DESERT STONE WAS YOUR HEART -
BUT BY MY HOLY SPIRIT -
BY MY SON'S LABOR OF LOVE -
THOU ART A DOOR UNTO EVERLASTING LIFE!
SO. BELOVED -
WHEN A TORMENTED SOUL COMES KNOCKING AT THE DOOR OF YOUR PULPIT WHEN A WOUNDED SOLDIER SAINT COMES KNOCKING AT THE DOOR OF YOUR HEART -
WHEN A HUNGRY SEEKING SOUL COMES -
ASKING FOR A DRINK OF LIFE -
LET THE EVERLASTING LIVING WATERS RISE UP FROM THY BELLY -
LET IT BE A FLOWING RIVER OF LIFE -
GIVING HOPE TO THE LOST -
GIVING THE HEALING BALM OF GILEAD TO THE WOUNDED -
GIVING FREEDOM TO THE CAPTIVES OF OUR ENEMY -
LET ALL COME TO THE PULPIT -
THERE MY SON SHALL BE THE LIGHT TO THE BLIND -
THERE MY SON SHALL BE THE WAY TO THE LOST -
THERE MY SON SHALL BE MY WORDS OF TRUTH TO THE SEEKERS OF JUSTICE AND RIGHTEOUSNESS!
THERE MY SON SHALL FEED THE MULTITUDE MANNA FROM THE HEAVENS -
THE NEW WINE OF MY HOLY SPIRIT SHALL BE GIVEN TO THOSE WHO THIRST FOR A COOL REFRESHING TOUCH IN THEIR MOST INNER CHAMBERS OF THEIR HEARTS.

ALL WHO HEAR THE BRIDEGROOM'S VOICE -
ALL THOSE WHO HEED HIS CALL -

ALL WHO COME AND PARTAKE OF THE WEDDING
FEAST - SHALL RECEIVE CROWNS OF EVERLASTING
LIFE! AND THE ENEMY SHALL BE DEFEATED - AND HIS
CHILDREN SHALL BE CAST OUT - FOR THEY SHALL BE
GNASHING THEIR TEETH IN TORMENT!

(*Footnote)
Praise the Lord! Glory and honor be to my God, forever and ever.
Amen!
Started this on 8/27/94 at 10:36 A.M. Finished this at 11:39 A.M.
Praise the Lord!!!

PATHS
BY THE HOLY SPIRIT

IN THIS WORLD THERE ARE MANY DIFFERENT PATHS -
THERE IS THE OVER-CROWDED FREEWAY -
THERE IS THE PEACEFUL WINDING COUNTRY ROAD -
THERE ARE PATHS TO AMUSEMENT CENTERS -
THERE ARE PATHS INTO A DENSE FOREST -
THERE ARE PATHS OF LIFE -
THERE ARE PATHS OF DESTRUCTION!

ONCE A MAN CAME INTO THIS WORLD,
HE WAS NOT A PHILOSOPHER -
HE WAS NOT A TEACHER -
HE WAS NOT A RABBI -
HE WAS NOT A SCRIBE -
HE WAS NOT A FISHERMAN -
YET -
HE WAS ALL THESE AND MUCH MORE!

HE WAS NOT A PHYSICIAN -
HE WAS NOT A CARPENTER -
HE WAS NOT EVEN A SOLDIER OF ANY WARRING
POWER OF THE TIME -
YET -
HE WAS ALL OF THESE AND MUCH MORE!

ONE DAY THIS MAN WALKED UPON COBBLE STREETS
TO ALL WHO CALLED HIM -
HE CAME AND VISITED WITH THAT CALLER!
TO THOSE WHO CALLED AND PLEADED FOR CLEANS-
ING AND HEALING -

HE WOULD CLEANSE AND HEAL!
TO THOSE WHO CALLED SEEKING WISDOM -
RECEIVED PARABLES THAT WOULD BRING THE LIS-
TENER BACK INTO HIS OWN IGNORANCE OR WOULD
SUDDENLY OPEN A WINDOW OF TRUTH AND UNDER-
STANDING!
THEY ALL KNEW HIM WELL -
YET -
THEY ALL KNEW HIM NOT!
FOR THIS MAN WAS A PARADOX UNTO THE INHABI-
TANTS OF THAT DAY!

ONE DAY HE SPOKE TO A GRAND MULTITUDE OF PEO-
PLE AND SAID UNTO THEM:
"ENTER THE GATES OF THE BROAD PATH -
"AND YOU WILL BE IN DEATH!"
"ENTER THRU THE NARROW GATE -"
"AND THERE WILL BE LIFE!"

ONE YOUNG MAN SAID:
"MASTER, I DO NOT UNDERSTAND! WHERE CAN I FIND
THIS NARROW GATE THAT LEADS TO LIFE?"
JESUS SMILED TO THE YOUNG MAN AND SOFTLY SAID:
"THESE GATES AND PATHS I SPEAK OF ARE NOT OF
THIS WORLD,
"YET, THEY ARE."
"FOR IF YOU HEED MY WORDS, WHICH ARE MY
FATHER'S WORDS,
"THEN YOU WILL HEAR AND SEE THE TRUTH FROM
THE HEART,"
"BUT, IF YOU DO NOT HEED MY WORDS,"
"THEN YOUR FATHER'S WORDS WILL BE SPOKEN INTO
YOUR HEART AND YOU "WILL BE LED ONTO THE
BROAD PATH AND THE GATE WILL LEAD INTO YOUR
FATHER'S KINGDOM OF EVERLASTING DEATH"!
ANOTHER MAN CRIED!

"MASTER, THESE WORDS THAT YOU SPEAK OF, WHO IS YOUR FATHER THAT WE MIGHT ALSO KNOW AND FOLLOW, FOR I TOO, SEEK AND DESIRE "THE PATH TO LIFE?"

JESUS LOOKED AT THE MULTITUDE SADLY, FOR MANY HAVE COME TO HEAR,
BUT MANY WERE DEAF TO HIS WORDS OF TRUTH!
THEN HE SPOKE THIS PARABLE TO THEM:
"THERE WERE TWO TRAVELERS WALKING ON THIS PATH TILL ALONG CAME A RICH WEALTHY MERCHANT."
"HE WAS ATTIRED IN THE FINEST GARMENTS,"
"HIS BEARD AND HAIR GLISTENED IN THE SUNLIGHT WITH THE FINEST "PERFUMED OILS."
"HIS FINGERS GLITTERED WITH MANY RINGS OF GOLD, DIAMONDS AND RARE GEMS.
WITH A BROAD SMILE, TEETH AS WHITE AS SNOW,"
"HE SPOKE AS SMOOTH AS SILK: 'WELL, MY FINE WEARY TRAVELERS!!
'COME WITH ME, I WILL SHOW YOU A PATH THAT WILL LEAD YOU TO FAME, FORTUNE, AND THE FINEST THAT LIFE HAS TO OFFER!'
"BUT JUST A FEW STEPS BEHIND THIS RICH MERCHANT, WAS ANOTHER "TRAVELER, THIS WAS A POOR SHEPHERD WITH A FEW OF HIS SHEEP."
"THIS ONE SPOKE SO SOFTLY AND GENTLE LIKE A SUMMER BREEZE:
'MY FRIENDS, DO NOT HEED HIS WORDS, FOR HE IS A ROBBER, HE WILL WORK "YOU TO HIS UNRELENTING WILL, YOU WILL BE IN BONDAGE TO HIM"
"AND IF YOU DO NOT DO HIS WILL, HE WILL OPPRESS YOU, AND YOU WILL "SEEK DEATH TO BE RELEASED FROM SUCH MISERABLE LIFE!"
"YET -
"COME!"

"FOLLOW ME"!
"I WILL GIVE YOU A WAY OF LIFE THAT YOU WILL FIND VERY LIGHT AND "REFRESHING!"
"COME!"
"LIVE WITH ME IN MY FATHER'S HOUSE!"
"TOGETHER, WE WILL CARE FOR YOU AND PROVIDE ALL THAT YOU WILL EVER "NEED!"
"I CANNOT GIVE YOU ALL THE FINERY THE FALSE MERCHANT OFFERS YOU,
"BUT, TO THOSE WHO FOLLOW ME, WILL NOT EVER NEED TO WORRY WHAT THE "NEXT DAY WILL BRING!"
"YOU WILL NOT NEED TO WORRY ABOUT WHERE YOU SHOULD LIVE OR WEAR OR WHAT YOU SHALL EAT, FOR MY FATHER TAKES CARE OF THE BIRDS IN THE SKY -
"SO SHALL HE TAKE CARE OF YOU!"
"IN ME, YOU WILL FIND FREEDOM FROM THIS WORLD'S BURDEN!"
"IN ME, YOU WILL FIND EVERLASTING LIFE!"

THE TWO TRAVELERS LOOKED AT ONE ANOTHER, ONE WENT WITH THE RICH MERCHANT, THE OTHER WENT WITH THE POOR SHEPHERD.

TIME PASSED ON!
THERE WERE TRAVELERS ON A PATH -
THERE WAS A RICH MERCHANT IN ALL HIS FINERY -
BUT, HE PULLED A HEAVY IRON CHAIN, TO WHOM WERE HIS SLAVES ATTACHED TO IT!
SO FRAIL AND WASTED WERE THESE WRETCHED SOULS!
CROSSING THE PATH OF THIS VILE RICH MERCHANT, WAS A SHEPHERD WITH HIS SHEEP,
AND FOLLOWING HIM WERE HIS BROTHERS WHO HELPED IN THE CARING OF THE SHEEP!

ONE OF THE WRETCHED SOULS CRIED OUT LOUDLY!
"MASTER, DO YOU REMEMBER ME?"
"I AM THAT TRAVELER YOU CALLED TO FOLLOW A LIFETIME AGO!"
" SAVE ME!"
" MASTER!"
"I SHOULD HAVE FOLLOWED YOU -
"BUT, I WAS SO DELUDED BY THE GRAND ILLUSION OF BECOMING WEALTHY, AS THIS ACCURSED MERCHANT PROMISED!"
THE SHEPHERD LOOKED AT THAT WRETCHED SOUL, TEARS FLOWED FROM HIS GENTLE VISAGE, HE SPOKE SO SOFTLY LIKE A GENTLE RAIN-DROP:
"MY SON -
"MANY I CALL TO FOLLOW ME"
"BUT -"
"FEW HEAR MY WORDS OF LIFE!"
"I HAVE CALLED YOU, MY SON -"
" YOU HEEDED NOT!"
"NOW FOR ALL ETERNITY YOU WILL SERVE THE MAS-TER YOU HAVE CHOSEN TO FOLLOW!

THE SHEPHERD, HIS BROTHERS AND HIS SHEEP WALKED ON - LEAVING THE WRETCHED SOUL WHO GNASHED HIS TEETH IN MISERY!

(*Footnote)
I received this in three parts, beginning July 2, 1990 at about 9:00 P.M. Then again on July 18, 1990 at about 12:00 A.M. Finally, finishing this on July 19,1990 around 2:00 P.M. Praise The Lord!

WATCHMAN'S ALERT!
BY THE HOLY SPIRIT.

BELOVED, SOUND THE TRUMPET!
AWAKE, MY CHILDREN!
MIDNIGHT IS UPON YOU!
FEAR NOT!
I AM WITH THEE!
OUR ENEMY ATTACKS MY LOST SHEEP -
THEY HAVE LOST THEIR TRUE SHEPHERD!
THERE ARE MANY FALSE SHEPHERDS WHO ARE GUID-
ING MY CHILDREN TO DESTRUCTION!
ARISE, BELOVED!
SOUND THE ALARM!
FOR GREAT IS THE DECEPTION THAT HAS FALLEN
UPON MY CHILDREN!
CRY, BELOVED -
FOR THEY HAVE BEEN BLINDED BY THE FALSE
REPORTS PEACE AND PROSPERITY!
O! JERUSALEM!
HAVE YOU NOT YET FOUND YOUR MESSIAH?
SEARCH NO LONGER -
FOR I WAS AMONG YOU -
YET -
YOU REJECTED ME!
FOR I CAME TO YOU AS A BEGGAR'S CHILD -
NOT A MIGHTY KING!
O! JERUSALEM!
YOUR MESSIAH IS AGAIN RETURNING -
WILL YOU RECEIVE YOUR KING?
OR WILL YOU REJECT HIM!
MY BELOVED BRIDE -

THE BATTLE IS UPON THEE -
STAND FIRM!
STAND VICTORIOUSLY!
SEE -
THE LION OF THE TRIBE OF JUDAH IS ROARING
ACROSS THE LAND!
THE HOLY SPIRIT'S WIND OF CHANGE IS SWEEPING
ACROSS THE RAGING WATERS!
THOSE WHO ARE IN THE ARK OF COVENANT WITH MY
FATHER -
SHALL BE KEPT IN CALM SEAS -
FOR THE FURIOUS ILL WIND OF THE ENEMY SHALL
NOT PREVAIL AGAINST MY PEOPLE!

WATCHMAN, WATCHMAN, ON THE TOWER GATE -
DO YOU SEE THE INVADING ARMIES OF HELL UPON
THEE?
SOUND THE TRUMPET LOUDLY!
NOW -
MY LIVING NEW JERUSALEM SHALL BE A GLORIOUS
PLACE OF REFUGE FOR ALL OF MY SCATTERED CHIL-
DREN!

I THEIR ONE AND ONLY TRUE KING -
SHALL CROWN THEM WITH CROWNS OF GLORY FOR
THEIR FAITHFULNESS IN ME!
SO. MY BELOVED -
BE AS A REED -
BEND WITH THE WIND OF MY HOLY SPIRIT -
YOU SHALL NOT BE BROKEN OR BRUISED -
RATHER YOU WILL BE STRENGTHENED -
SO THAT WHEN THE WINDS OF HATE COME RUSHING
AGAINST THEE -
YOU WILL NOT BE UPROOTED AND LOST!
HEAR MY VOICE, BELOVED -
FOR ONLY THOSE WHO ARE TRULY MINE -

WILL HEAR THE VOICE OF THEIR MASTER -
AND THE STUDENT WITH A GLAD HEART WILL DESIRE
THE WISDOM OF THE TEACHER.

SO BELOVED -
LET US BE A HOUSE THAT IS WELL FOUNDED -
WHERE THE CORNERSTONE IS FIRMLY ANCHORED IN
THE FOUNDATION OF FAITH THIS IS THY STRENGTH -
THIS IS THY JOY -
THAT AS THE ENEMY RAVAGES ALL AROUND YOU -
NO HARM, NO DESTRUCTION WILL FALL UPON YOU!
SEEK NOT THE FALSE TEACHERS WHO WILL SHOW
YOU A PATH FRAUGHT WITH DANGERS -
FOR THEY ARE WOLVES IN SHEEP'S CLOTHING -
THEY ONLY SEEK FOR THEIR OWN DESIRES OF
WEALTH AND ADMIRATION YET -
BE NOT DECEIVED BY THEIR WORDS OF FLOWERY
WISDOM -
SEEK THE WORD THAT WASHES AND REFRESHES YOUR
SPIRIT FROM THE VENOM OF THE ENEMY'S BITE!
BE NOT AFRAID -
DEATH WILL HAVE NO HOLD UPON YOU -
I HAVE TAKEN HIS STING AWAY!

SO, BELOVED -
HEED WELL THE WATCHMAN'S TRUMPET CALL -
HE IS ANNOUNCING THAT THE MASTER OF THE HOUSE
IS RETURNING!
GREAT WILL BE HIS REWARD TO THE SERVANTS WHO
KEPT HIS COMMANDS AND DID HIS WILL!
NOW, BELOVED -
I CLOTHE THEE IN GARMENTS OF SNOW WHITE LINEN
NO BLEMISHES, NO STAINS, NO WRINKLES -
PURE AS GOLD MANY TIMES REFINED SHALT THOU BE -
FOR ALL TO WITNESS MY BELOVED BRIDE!

(*Footnote)
Praise the Lord! Glory to God on high! Started this on 2/20/94, at
9:10 A.M. Finished this at 9:35 A.M. Praise the Lord!

PROPHECY 11/16/92

OH! MY BELOVED!
HAVE NO FEAR!
BUT ARISE!
FOR NOW IS THE TIME FOR REJOICING -
FOR NOW THE HOLY SPIRIT IS HOVERING OVER THE
STILL WATERS OF YOUR LIFE -
SO AWAKE, MY BELOVED!
BE MY BRIDE -
SOUND THE BATTLE TRUMPET -
FOR I YOUR BRIDEGROOM IS COMING TO RESCUE YOU
FROM THE STRONGHOLD OF THE ENEMY!
SO, BELOVED -
COME IN JOYOUS SONG -
COME IN GLORIOUS VICTORY!
FOR THE ENEMY MUST FLEE -
THE MORNING OF REDEMPTION IS NEAR AT HAND!

SELAH!

PATHS OF LIGHT PATHS OF DARKNESS A REVELATION BY THE HOLY SPIRIT

AS WE TRAVEL THE HIGHWAYS AND BYWAYS OF LIFE,
WE COME TO MANY CROSSROADS -
THERE BEFORE US WE MUST MAKE A CHOICE -
EITHER THE ROAD ON THE LEFT -
OR THE ROAD ON THE RIGHT!

THE ROAD ON THE LEFT IS QUITE BROAD -
THE ROAD ON THE RIGHT IS QUITE NARROW -
THE ROAD ON THE LEFT IS QUITE TRAVELED -
THE ROAD ON THE RIGHT IS QUITE DESERTED!
SO IN MY DAYS OF INNOCENCE,
I CHOSE THE PATH ON THE LEFT,
FOR SURELY IF I NEEDED GUIDANCE THERE WOULD
BE QUITE A FEW ROAD-WISE TRAVELERS!

SO ONWARD ONTO THE BROAD PATH I SET MY FEET
UPON -
THERE WAS A CROWD OF PEOPLE -
JOYOUSLY LAUGHING AND CAROUSING -
"COME FOLLOW US!"
THEY JOVIALLY SPOKE TO ME
THEY SPRINTING DOWN THE PATH,
CAUGHT ME UP IN THE RAUCOUS REVELRY!
TILL WE CAME UPON AN OLD MAN -
HOW THEY TRIED TO COAX HIM INTO OUR COMPANY!
YET -
WITH LIVING WORDS SPEWED VEHEMENTLY AT HIM,
THE LIVING WORDS FELL DEAD AT HIS FEET!
HOW THEY JEERED AND MOCKED HIM!

THEN THEY BEGAN TO TORMENT HIM WITH THEIR
VILE WORDS -
AND WITH EACH POISONOUS WORD INFLICTED UPON
THIS POOR SOUL,
THE OLD MAN GREW WEAKER,
HIS WORDS FLICKERED DESPERATELY FOR LIFE -
BUT THIS COMPANY OF MALICIOUS SPIRITS DELIGHT-
ED IN HIS PAIN AND HUMILIATION!
ALL. OF A SUDDEN -
A WELLSPRING OF MERCY AND COMPASSION OVER-
WHELMED ME,
AND I BEGAN TO BESEECH THESE EVIL SPIRITS TO
LEAVE HIM AND GO THEIR WAY -
BUT THEY BEGAN TO TURN ON ME!
THEIR POISONOUS DARTS PIERCED ME AND I FELT THE
GRIP OF DEATH UPON ME!
THE OLD MAN CRIED OUT "RUN LITTLE ONE!"
"RUN TOWARDS THE NARROW PATH -
"THERE YOU WILL FIND TRUE HAPPINESS!
"REMEMBER ME, LITTLE ONE, WHEN YOU SEE THE
KING ABOVE ALL KINGS!"

AND SO I RAN, BUT LIKE WOLVES THEY SNAPPED AT
MY HEELS I LOOKED TO AND FRO FOR THE NARROW
PATH,
BUT IT WAS NOWHERE IN SIGHT!
I BEGAN TO CRY IN DESPAIR!
"OH! KING OF ALL KINGS!"
"IF YOU CAN ONLY HEAR MY CRY FOR HELP!"
"I CHOSE THE WRONG PATH -
"YOUR PATH WAS SO VERY NARROW,
"I DID NOT SEE ANY TRAVELERS ALONG THAT PATH,
"AND I FEARED TO GO ALONE WITHOUT A COMPANION!"
"HELP ME! OH! LORD!"
"I PROMISE I WILL STAY ON YOUR PATH,
"AND BE A GUARDIAN TO WARN ALL THOSE WHO

COME TO THE CROSSROADS OF THEIR LIVES -
"THAT THOUGH THERE BE TWO PATHS,
"ONLY THE TRUE WAY LEADS TO LIFE WITH YOU!"
"THE OTHER PATH, APPEALING TO THE SENSES,
"IS BUT A FALSE ROAD THAT ONLY LEADS TO FOREVER
TORMENT!"
"AND I WILL CALL TO THE WANDERERS TO COME ON
THE RIGHT PATH,
"JUST AS THE OLD MAN HAS DONE FOR ME!"

THEN SUDDENLY BEFORE ME
THERE WAS A GOLDEN PATH,
AND I HEARD A GENTLE CALM VOICE IN MY HEART -
"COME, MY LITTLE ONE!"
"FOR I SHALL MAKE YOU MY CROSSROAD TO
MANKIND!"
"COME, MY BELOVED LITTLE ONE!"
"I HAVE GREAT NEED AND URGENCY TO HAVE YOU
HOLD MY LIGHT ON THESE PATHS -
"FOR DARKNESS HAS DESCENDED AND MY PEOPLE
ARE IN FEAR -
"THEY SEEK, NOT KNOWING WHAT THEY SEEK -
"YET -
"THEY CRY OUT UNTO ME TO SAVE THEM!"
"SO, MY LITTLE CHOSEN ONE -
"I WILL GIVE YOU THE FIRE OF MY HOLY SPIRIT AS
YOUR COMPANION AND GUIDE -
"HEED HIM WELL!"
"LET MY LIGHT BE A LAMP UNTO THY FEET!"
"FOR IT IS TIME FOR MY PEOPLE TO COME TO THEIR
TRUE HOME!"

(*Footnote)
Praise the Lord!!!! Amen!!!! To God be the glory!!!
This was given to me on 1/29/91, started this at 9.00 A.M. during
my break time. Ended at 9:15 A.M. Started again at 11:40 A.M.

during my lunch time, ended at 12:12 P.M.
While I typed this Jesus spoke to me and really finished this revelation! Praise the Lord!!!

STONE MAID - MAID OF HONOR!

"FAIR MAIDENS, PRAY TELL ME, WHERE ARE YOU TRAVELING THIS FINE DAY?"
ONE. MAIDEN, WHOSE VISAGE WAS A STERN LOOK OF BEING ADDRESSED BY A STRANGER!
ONE MAIDEN, WHOSE VISAGE WAS AS FAIR AS AN ANGEL FROM THE HEAVENS ABOVE!
THIS YOUNG MAID, WHOSE SWEET VOICE WAS A MELODY OF JOY, SPOKE TO ME:
"SIR! MAY OUR LORD BLESS YOUR TRAVEL! WE ARE GOING TO OUR MASTER'S HOME -
"THERE IS AN INVITATION TO A MARRIAGE FEAST, HAVE YOU RECEIVED HIS CALL?"
THE STONEY-MAID, WHOSE HAUGHTY VOICE STUNG AS A POISONOUS ASP -
"SIR! YOU HAVE NO MANNERS OF A GENTLEMAN! HOW DARE YOU ADDRESS US AS THOUGH WE ARE YOUR FAMILIAR EQUALS?"
WITH BITING, LASHING WORDS SHE SCOLDED THE FAIR MAIDEN FOR SPEAKING TO ME!

THERE CAME A FORK IN THE PATH OF THESE TWO MAIDENS,
THE FAIR BEAUTY EAGERLY POINTED TO HER RIGHT -
THE STONE-HEARTED MAIDEN ARGUED THE RIGHT CHOICE WAS TO GO ON THE LEFT ROAD!
AS THEY WERE DISCUSSING WHAT CHOICE TO MAKE - TWO TRAVELERS APPROACHED THEM, ONE CAME FROM THE LEFT PATH,
THE OTHER FROM THE RIGHT PATH!
THE TRAVELER FROM THE LEFT PATH WAS AN ARRO-

GANT WELL-LEARNED GENTLEMAN,
THE TRAVELER FROM THE RIGHT PATH WAS A POOR
SHEPHERD LAD WITH A FEW OF HIS SHEEP!
THE SEEMINGLY RICH TRAVELER ADDRESSED THE
TWO MAIDENS:
"MY FOOLISH BEAUTIES! WHAT CAN BE DISMAYING
SO DEEPLY AMONGST THEE?"
THE MAID OF STONE RASPED IN A TONE OF DIGNITY
"SIR! MY SISTER AND I ARE SEEKING THE LORD'S CAS-
TLE!
"THERE IS A MARRIAGE FEAST BEING CELEBRATED
THIS DAY!
"I DEFINITELY KNOW THE CORRECT PATH TO TAKE,
"BUT MY FOOLISH SISTER IS INSISTING THE PATH I
CHOSE IS INCORRECT!"

"PLEASE SIR, CAN YOU DIRECT US? I NOTICED THAT
YOU HAVE COME FROM THE DIRECTION I CHOSE TO
TAKE!"
THE POOR SHEPHERD GENTLY SPOKE:
"YOUR FAIR SISTER HAS SPOKEN CORRECTLY,
"FOR HER HEART KNOWS HER LORD'S HOME!"
THE MAID OF STONE, WITH A DISDAINED LOOK AT THE
POOR SHEPHERD, HISSED LIKE A SNAKE, HER MEA-
SURED VOICE, DRIPPING WITH VENOM:
FROM WHENCE THOU CAME, I CAN SEE YOUR MAS-
TER'S HOME IS NOT FIT FOR HUMAN HABITATION!
"GO BACK TO YOUR HOVEL OF FILTH!"
WITH A COLD STERN VOICE SHE ADDRESSED HER SISTER:
"YOU SHALL FOLLOW ME, FOR I KNOW THE MASTER'S
HOUSE!
"SEE HOW REFINED THIS TRAVELER IS?"
"OUR MASTER IS NO POOR FILTHY HERDSMAN!"
THE FAIR MAIDEN, WHOSE INNER GLOW FOR THE
LOVE OF HER LORD BLUSHED AS A ROSE KISSED BY
DEW -

"SISTER, DO NOT BE DECEIVED, OUR LORD'S ENEMIES ARE CUNNING, THEY ARE LIARS, THIEVES AND MUR-DERERS!"

"MY SOUL IS TROUBLED WHEN I GAZE UPON THE RICH TRAVELER -

"OH! HOW MY SOUL LEAPS FOR JOY WHEN I GAZE UPON THIS POOR SHEPHERD!"

"COME, MY BELOVED SISTER, LET US TRAVEL THE PATH OF THIS SHEPHERD LAD!"

WITH A SHRUG OF INDIFFERENCE TO HER SISTER'S PLEA, SHE TOOK HOLD OF THE RICH TRAVELER'S HAND AND TOGETHER, THEY COMMENCED TO WALK THE PATH TO THEIR LEFT!

THE SHEPHERD LOOKED WITH EYES FULL OF LOVE FOR THE MAID WHO CHOSE TO FOLLOW HIM -

IN A TWINKLING OF A MOMENT, THE POOR SHEPHERD WAS NO MORE!

THERE AT THE PATH TO THE RIGHT WAS A SPLENDID GLORIOUS KING!

WITH A VOICE AS GENTLE AS A SUMMERS BREEZE, HE CALLED UNTO HER:

"COME, MY BELOVED MAID OF HONOR, LET US GO TO THE MARRIAGE FEAST,

"FOR I HAVE AT LAST FOUND MY ONE TRUE BRIDE!"

(*Footnote)

Praise the Lord! Started this on 4/12/97 at 7:50 P.M. finished intermittently between work at 8:50 P. M I hear the voice of my Holy Spirit deep within the chambers of my heart - Reader, He questions about the temple that is within thee, are you a cold stone maid - or are you His resplendent temple of glory - are you His fair maid of honor? Reader, beware of the enemy that would make you callous to our Lord's calling!

AMEN!

CLOUDS ON A STORMY HORIZON

COME, MY BELOVED!
FRET NOT!
DO NOT BE FAINT-HEARTED -
FEAR NOT!
THOUGH THE ENEMY IS FIERCE -
THOUGH THERE BE STORMS AND TEMPESTS THAT
SEEM TO CAPTURE YOUR VERY SOUL -
REJOICE!
FOR IN THE TEMPEST -
YOU WILL SEE MY GLORY!

COME, MY BELOVED!
COME INTO THE SECRET PLACE
COME INTO THE GARDEN -
COME AND REST WITH ME!

REMEMBER, MY BELOVED -
THOUGH THIS EARTH WILL PASS AWAY MY WORDS ARE
LIFE EVERLASTING UNTO THEE!
HAVE I NOT SPOKEN THAT NO ONE CAN TAKE THEE
AWAY FROM ME!
I HAVE CHOSEN YOU!
YOU WOULD NOT HAVE CHOSEN ME -
YET -
I LAID MY LIFE DOWN FOR YOU -
SO THAT YOU WILL HAVE MY SPIRIT WITHIN THEE!

SO COME, MY BELOVED!
COME DANCING BEFORE ME WITH JOY AND ABANDON
THYSELF AS DAVID DANCED TO HIS LORD!

COME SINGING PRAISES, BELOVED -
I DO NOT NEED TO HAVE YOUR PRAISES -
YET -
IN PRAISE LIES YOUR STRENGTH AND VICTORY OVER
THE ENEMY'S WEAPONS AGAINST THEE!

SEE! BELOVED - THE STORM CLOUDS AT THE HORIZON
OF YOUR LIFE - DRAW ME CLOSER TO THEE - JUST AS
MY FOLLOWERS CRIED OUT -
"LORD! -
SAVE US!"

COME, MY BELOVED!
COME TO THE SHORES OF GALILEE LET US SUP
TOGETHER -
FOR IN FELLOWSHIP -
THE GATES OF HELL CANNOT AND WILL NOT PREVAIL
AGAINST THEE!
REMEMBER -
I HAVE SPOKEN -
NEVER WILL I LEAVE YOU -
THOUGH YE BE THROUGH THE FIRE -
THE ENEMY DOES NOT HAVE THE VICTORY -
FOR I ON CALVARY, BY MY SHED BLOOD -
VICTORY HAS BEEN PROCLAIMED!
I AM YOUR SHEPHERD -
I WILL LEAD YOU TO GREEN PASTURES -
FOR I HAVE PLANS FOR THEE -
NOT EVIL -
BUT GOOD PLANS FOR YOUR TOMORROW'S -
TRUST IN ME, LEAN NOT TO THY OWN UNDERSTANDING -
AND YOU SHALL BE MY WITNESS FOR ALL TO SEE MY
GLORY THROUGH YOU!

(*Footnote) Praise the Lord! Received this on 3/21/94 at 10:00
A.M.

PROPHECY 1 1/29/92

OH! COME, MY BELOVED CHILDREN!
THERE IS A FAMINE FALLING UPON THIS LAND!
THE WILDERNESS IS OVERCOMING THE FERTILE LAND!
THE ENEMY SEEKS AND HE DESTROYS -
YET -
FEAR NOT! MY BELOVED -
FOR DEEP IN ME, THE WATERS OF LIFE ARE STILL
FLOWING -
SO COME REFRESH YOURSELVES -
DRINK DEEPLY OF ME -
FOR IN THIS DAY -
FOR IN THIS HOUR -
THE ANGELIC HOSTS ARE MINISTERING AND BAT-
TLING WITH YOU!
HAVE I NOT SPOKEN: 'I WILL NEVER FORSAKE THEE...!
MY BELOVED CHILDREN -
THERE ARE THOSE OF MY CHILDREN THAT ARE LOST,
THAT DO NOT KNOW OF ME,
THERE ARE THOSE WHO HAVE REJECTED ME -
FOR SUCH AS THESE, BELOVED -
YOU AND I MUST REACH OUT IN LOVING MERCY AND
SHOW THEM THE WAY TO THE SHORES OF SAFETY AND
FREEDOM!
SO, COME!
DRINK AND REFRESH THYSELVES IN MY HOLY SPIRIT -
THE WORK IS GREAT, PRAY FOR THE LABORERS -
LET MY HOLY SPIRIT GUIDE YOU AND HEAL YOU FOR
EACH MOMENT OF HOPE IS POURED OUT UPON THEE!

(*Footnote) Received this 11/29/92, Praise the Lord!

THE TIDES OF WAR!

IN THE DISTANT -
ROLLS OF DRUMBEAT MUFFLED BEAT -
LIKE A TIDAL WAVE -
ITS LIFE SURGES EVER STRONGER FORWARD -
WAR!
WAR!
WAR!

IN THE DISTANT -
THE EARTH TREMBLES!
A GIANT TRODS UPON HER DUSTY PLAINS -
DO YOU HEAR HIS WAR CRY!
IN THE RISING WIND -
A GALE FORCE OF ANGER AND HATRED -
BLOWS ACROSS THE WILDERNESS!
THE RISING WIND SCREECHES THE GIANT'S WAR CRY:
"ENEMY!"
"YOU SHALL DIE BY MY SWORD!"

DO NOT FEAR!
DO NOT TREMBLE!
THERE IN THE HORIZON -
IN THE ROLLING STORM CLOUDS OF HATRED -
THE SON IS ARISING!
GREATER AND MIGHTIER IS HIS BATTLE CHALLENGE!
FOR HE IS THE MIGHTY KING -
THE LION OF THE TRIBE OF JUDAH!
ALL THE NATIONS -
ALL THE PEOPLE -
HOW THEY COWER IN FEAR -

FOR WITH THE GIANT, THEY MARCHED AGAINST THIS
MIGHTY KING'S PEOPLE!
BUT IN THE CHANGING WIND -
A WIND OF LIFE SURGES -
THE WILDERNESS SPRINGS FORTH WITH LIFE!

OUT OF THE THORNY BUSHES -
ROSES BLOOM! OUT OF THE PARCHED DUSTY EARTH -
MIGHTY CEDARS RISE TO THE HEAVENS! OUT OF THE
FLATLAND -
A MIGHTY MOUNTAIN RISES -
THE MOUNTAIN CALLED -
ZION! HERE IS THE KING'S KINGDOM -
SEE HIS PEOPLE DANCE AND SING IN VICTORY!
SEE THE SCOUTS OF THE ENEMY RUN IN FEAR!

LOOK BEYOND THE STORMS OF WAR -
LOOK BEYOND THE HORDE OF ENEMIES -
SET YOUR EYES UPON THE MOUNT OF YOUR KING'S
GLORY -
SEE THE CRIMSON BANNER -
SEE THE SNOW WHITE LAMB OF GOD -
SET IN THE CRIMSON BACKGROUND OF THE KING'S
BANNER OF LOVE!

SO, COME!
WIPE AWAY THOSE TEARS OF DESPERATION!
PUT OFF THE SACKCLOTHS OF MOURNING -
PUT ON THE GARMENTS OF GLADNESS -
FOR THE SON IS COMING -
HIS BRIDE HE WILL CLAIM -
NO LONGER CAN HIS ENEMY LAY CLAIM UPON HER -
FOR WITH HIS LIFE, HE RANSOMED HIS BELOVED!
SO, PEOPLE OF THE EARTH -
DO NOT TREMBLE AT THE GIANT'S ROAR -
DO NOT FEAR!

ARE YOU THE MIGHTY KING'S BRIDE?
OR ARE YOU THE CHILDREN OF DARKNESS?
IF YE BE THE CHOSEN ONE -
REJOICE!
IF YE BE THE KING'S ENEMY -
BEWARE!
FOR HE COMES IN JUDGEMENT
BEARING REWARDS AND CROWNS FOR HIS BELOVED -
BEARING WRATH AND VENGEANCE TO HIS ENEMIES!

(*Footnote)
Praise the Lord! Started this at work 11/30/94 at 12:30 P.M.
Finished this at 2:10 P.M.
Glory to my King above all kings - Jesus Christ of Nazareth!

RIDERS IN THE SKY

IN THE STILLNESS OF THE AIR -
CLOUDS RUSHED TOGETHER IN ANGRY SWIRLS -
A DISTANT RUMBLING CAN BE HEARD -
SPEARS OF LIGHTNING WERE THRUST EARTHWARD! IN
THE MIDST OF THESE THUNDEROUS CLOUDS -
I HEARD THE DISTANT BEAT OF MANY HOOVES -
BY THE GROWING RUMBLE UPON THE PREGNANT SKY -
MY HEART FROZE AT THE SIGHT OF THESE TERRIBLE
RIDERS!

THE FIRST WAS A RIDER ON A WHITE HORSE -
IT'S RIDER HELD A BOW -
AND HE WAS WEARING A CROWN OF CONQUEST!
BEHIND THIS RIDER WAS A FIERY RED ONE -
IT'S RIDER CARRIED A LARGE SWORD!
BEHIND THIS RIDER WAS A BLACK HORSE -
IT'S RIDER WAS HOLDING A PAIR OF SCALES IN HIS
MIGHTY GLOVED HAND!
BEHIND THIS RIDER WAS A PALE HORSE -
IT'S RIDER WAS NAMED -

DEATH!
AND ALMOST ABREAST THIS RIDER -
HADES WAS FOLLOWING CLOSE BEHIND!
THE HORSE WAS BELLOWING FORTH FROM HIS
FLARED NOSTRILS -
HIS FOOLISH BREATH ACROSS THE STORMY SKY!
THESE GRIM RIDERS GALLOPED UPON THE SURGING
UPDRAFT WINDS OF DESPAIR AND HOPELESSNESS -
THAT WAS RISING UP FROM THE EARTH FAR BELOW!

WITH A SET PURPOSE -
THEY RODE AT A FURIOUS SPEED!

THE FIRST RIDER -
DIVIDED THE PEOPLES AMONGST THE VARIOUS
NATIONS AND TRIBES -
THOSE WHO WERE THE WILLING SERVANTS TO THIS
TERRIBLE CONQUEROR -
RECEIVED HIS MUCH SOUGHT FAVOR AND GIFTS!
TO THE REBELLIOUS PEOPLE WHO WOULD NOT WILL-
INGLY SERVE HIM -
FROM HIS MIGHTY BOW, HE WOULD SHOOT DOWN
FIERY BOLTS AMONGST THEMSELVES!
THIS CAUSED CONFUSION, JEALOUSY AND HATRED
TOWARDS THE WILLING SERVANTS OF THIS AWESOME
AND FEARSOME MASTER!

THE SECOND RIDER CARRIED A LARGE DOUBLE-EDGED
BROAD SWORD -
HE CLEAVED MIGHTY SWATHS OF SUSPICION AND DIS-
TRUST AMONGST THE VARIOUS NATIONS AND TRIBES -
AND THEY BEGAN TO SLAUGHTER ONE ANOTHER!

THE THIRD RIDER WAS THE HARVESTER -
IN HIS ONE MIGHTY GLOVED HAND, HE CARRIED A
SICKLE!
IN HIS OTHER HAND, HE CARRIED THE FULL JUST MEA-
SURE THAT WAS GIVEN TO HIM ACCORDING TO HIS
SIGHT AND ACCORDING TO HIS PLEASURE -
THE DESERVING AND THE RIGHTEOUS SERVANTS OF
THIS MIGHTY MASTER -
WERE THEN WITH A MIGHTY CUTTING SWOOP OF HIS
SICKLE -
HE WOULD GATHER THE BLACKENED TARES -
THEN WITH A HOT BRANDISHING IRON -
HE WOULD SEAL THESE SERVANTS FROM THE HAR-

VEST WITH HIS MARK UNTIL THE FINAL HARVEST!

THE FOURTH RIDER WAS THE MOST HORRID OF ALL!
FOR HE BROUGHT THE DRYING WINDS OF DEATH TO
THIS LAND FAR BELOW!
AS THIS SIROCCO WIND BLEW ACROSS THE EARTH -
ACROSS THE MIGHTY FORESTS -
ACROSS THE PLAINS OF BLUE-GREEN GRASS THAT
SWAYED IN THE GENTLE BREEZES -
ACROSS THE RIBBONS AND POOLS AND SEAS THAT
SWIRLED AND INTERTWINED WITH THE LAND -
HE BROUGHT THE DRYING WINDS OF DEATH TO THE
LAND FAR BELOW -
WHERE NO GRASS OR TREES OR PLAINS OR MEADOWS
COULD EVER GROW AGAIN!
WHERE THE LAKES AND RIVERS AND STREAMS AND
CREEKS GAVE UP THEIR LIFE-SUSTAINING MOISTURE
AND COOLNESS OF ATMOSPHERE, ONLY TO BECOME A
VAST PART OF THE EVER-GROWING ARID WASTE-
LANDS AND DESERTS!
HE CALLED THE WILD BEASTS TO ATTACK AND
SLAUGHTER THE PEOPLE WHO HAD HUNTED AND
RUTHLESSLY SLAUGHTERED THEM!
HE WHISTLED AT THE LOCUST TO EAT THE ALLOWED
MEASURE FROM THE HARVEST -
HOW THE PEOPLE OF THIS EARTH DIED FROM THE
LACK OF NOURISHMENT AND SUSTENANCE A GREAT
THIRST AROSE FROM THEIR SEARED MOUTHS -
"SET US FREE!" THEY CRIED TO THE UNHEEDING
WINDS OF DEATH!
HE ALSO CALLED TO THE MALIGNANT LIFE THAT
DWELLED IN THEIR FAST DRYING WATERS OF LIFE -
AND THAT DWELLED IN THE EARTH -
TO BRING DOWN DISEASES TO THE CATTLE AND
AMONGST THE VARIOUS NATIONS AND AS THESE
POOR WITHERED PEOPLE PERISHED -

FROM THE PATH OF DEATH AND DESTRUCTION OF THE THIRD RIDER -

HADES -

QUICKLY GATHERED THE FEAST AND GORGED ITSELF TO A WANTON FRENZY OF GLUTTONY!

WAS IT THUNDER THAT I HEARD? OR WAS IT THOSE FEARSOME RIDERS IN THE SKY - RIDING UPON THE STORM CLOUDS OF APOCALYPSE TO THE FOUR CORNERS OF THIS DYING PLANET!

"LORD!"
"HAVE MERCY ON EACH AND EVERY SOUL UPON THIS PLANET!"
"IN THE MIGHTY AND HOLY PRECIOUS NAME OF YOUR BELOVED SON -
"JESUS CHRIST OF NAZARETH -
"HAVE MERCY ON US!"

(*Footnote)
Received this vision in 8/90, while there was a threatening storm in Minnesota! Now 6/28/94, here in New Jersey, the Lord renews and refinishes this awesome vision! Praise God! Amen! Started this on 6/28/94 at 11:18 P.M. Finished this at 12:12A.M.

ACID RAIN -
LATTER RAIN!

UPDRAFTS OF MOISTURE RISING TO THE HEAVENS -
IN MIST OF STEAM FROM TEMPERATURES UNBEARING -
SOFT BILLOWY STREAMS STREAK THE HEAVENS SO
BLUE!

DENSE MOUNTAINS OF CLOUDS RISING INTO THE
HEAVENS -
WITHIN -
THERE SEEMS TO BE A BLACK SWIRL OVERTAKING
THIS MOUNTAIN IN THE SKY!
DEEP WITHIN -
FLASHES BEAM ROUND THE MOUNTAIN -
THUNDER SEEMS TO BE ITS VOICE -
FIRST ONE -
THEN MANY!
AS A CHORUS OF ANGRY FLASHES ARE THROWN FROM
ONE MOUNTAIN TO ANOTHER!
AND ITS DENIZENS THAT DWELL WITHIN GRUMBLE
THEIR VEXATION OF MISSING THE ENEMY!
LIQUID ARROWS ARE PELTED UPON THE INNOCENT
EARTH FAR BELOW!
THE ENEMY FILLED THESE DROPLETS WITH ITS
ACIDIC HATRED TOWARDS THE BEINGS WHO DWELL
IN THE LAND FAR BELOW!

IN HOUSES OF STRAW -
IN SHABBY SHANTIES -
IN MANSIONS SO GRAND -
MAN STRUGGLES WITH THE STORM RAGING DEEP

WITHIN HIS HEART!

IN A CARDBOARD HOUSE IN A DIRTY ALLEY -
MAN HUDDLES HIS FEW SQUANDERED BELONGINGS
AS THOUGH THEY WERE TREASURES OF UNTOLD
WEALTH!

IN HOUSES OF STRAW -
MAN CHALLENGES HIS FELLOW TRIBESMEN FOR THE
RIGHT TO LIVE -
FOR HE IS A MIGHTY HUNTER, WARRIOR, ONE TO BE
FEARED OF!

IN MANSIONS SO GRAND -
MAN MUST RULE AND DOMINATE THE WORLD!
OR THERE IS HELL TO PAY FOR!
FOR HE IS ALL MIGHTY -
FOR HE IS ALL POWERFUL -
SEE HOW GREAT HIS ARMY IS!
SEE HOW NUMEROUS THEY ARE!
LIKE LOCUSTS IN A FIELD OF GOLDEN WHEAT IN A
FEEDING FRENZY -
ALL LIFE IS WIPED OUT!
ONLY STUBBLE REMAINS WERE THERE ONCE WAS A
GOLDEN SEA OF WHEAT!
SO TOO LIKE POISONOUS ACID-FILLED ARROWS THEY
AIM AT ONE ANOTHER THEIR ANGER AND THEIR LUST!
MAN CRINGES -
YET HE IS READY TO POUNCE UPON YOU AND TEAR
YOU APART!

YET -
IN ALL THIS CHAOS OF MURDER, GREED AND PRIDE -
THERE IS HOPE!
FOR WE HAVE A COVENANT WRITTEN IN THE HEAVENS
ABOVE A RAINBOW IN THE STORM-VENTED SKY -

THAT THERE IS A GOD WHO IS LOVE TO HIS CHILDREN!
IN HIS LIVING WORD, WE HAVE HIS SEAL -
BY HIS MIGHT, BY HIS POWER, BY HIS HOLY SPIRIT -
WE ARE GIVEN THE ANTIDOTE FROM DEATH -
JESUS OF NAZARETH!
HE IS OUR LATTER RAIN!
AS A GARDEN NEEDING TENDER LOVING CARE -
HE SETS UPON HIS TASK WITH JOY!
HE GIVES US GENTLE RAIN -
HE NOURISHES AND STRENGTHENS OUR ROOTS WITH
THE MANNA FROM HIS FATHER'S TABLE!
COME!
RECEIVE THE ANTIDOTE FROM THE ENEMIES ACID
RAIN -
RECEIVE OUR LORD'S LATTER RAIN OF LIFE!

(*Footnote)
Praise God! Started this 8:00 P.M. Finished this at 8:20 P.M.
Praise The Lord!

FAMINE IN THE WASTELANDS BY THE HOLY SPIRIT

OPENED MY BIBLE TO JOEL, I WAS PRAYING FOR A TEACHING.

THE LORD IS RE-EMPHASIZING THAT WE "JUDAH" ARE IN THE JUDGMENT.

WE ARE IN THAT GREAT AND AWESOME DAY OF THE LORD!

I WAS READING THE INTRODUCTION ABOUT JOEL'S DESCRIPTION OF WHAT THE PLAGUE OF LOCUST HAVE DONE -

WHEN SUDDENLY I HAD A VISION -

HERE NOW BEGINS THE JOURNEY INTO THAT GREAT AND AWESOME DAY OF THE LORD!

"HERE I AM, LORD -
"PEN READY TO MARK DOWN YOUR TEACHING -
"PEN READY TO OBSERVE THE LESSON-"
THE ROOM IS STILL -
THE BREEZE IS STILL -
THERE'S AN EXPECTANCY ALL AROUND ME -
QUIETLY -
I SILENTLY PRAY -
"JESUS OF NAZARETH, MY LORD -
"I WELCOME YOUR SWEET PRESENCE -
"LORD, I AM HERE,
"SPEAK TO YOUR SERVANT -
"WHAT IS GRIEVING YOU, MY SWEET JESUS OF NAZARETH?"

SUDDENLY!

THE ROOM IS FILLED WITH A PROFUSE AROMA OF A COUNTRY GARDEN!

THE GENTLE RUSTLING OF THE EVENING BREEZE CARESSED MY WARM COUNTENANCE -

I LOOKED UP FROM THIS WRITING -

YES!

THERE BY MY WINDOW -

STOOD MY SWEET PRECIOUS LORD!

HIS PRESENCE FILLED TO OVERFILLING MY TINY ROOM!

HOW MY HEART RACED!

I LOOKED UPON HIS GLORIOUS VISAGE -

THERE WAS A STERN, SOMBER APPEARANCE -

HIS EYES WERE LIKE STEEL BLUE BOLTS OF LIGHT-NING -

HIS WAVY HAIR GLISTENED AS THOUGH PEARLS WERE INTERTWINED IN HIS BURNISHED LOCKS!

UPON HIS BROW, A BRILLIANT GOLDEN STAR-STUD-DED CROWN ENCIRCLED HIS HEAD.

A GARMENT OF BLUE, IT APPEARS HE HAS CLOTHED HIMSELF IN THE NOONDAY SKY!

A DEWY SPUN GARMENT OF SNOW-WHITE WAS BENEATH THE OVER-COAT,

ROUND ABOUT HIM, A BELT OF GOLDEN THREADS ENCIRCLED HIS WAIST,

GOLDEN NET-LIKE SANDALS COVERED HIS FEET.

IN A SOFT VOICE -

A VOICE AS THAT OF A GENTLE BREATH OF AIR, HE SPOKE TO HIS SERVANT:

"COME!"

"FOLLOW ME!"

IMMEDIATELY, I AROSE FROM MY BED, JOYFULLY I CLASPED MY TINY HAND INTO HIS STRONG TENDER

HAND -
WE STEPPED OUTSIDE INTO THE COOLNESS OF THE
NIGHT -
WE SILENTLY GLIDED OVER BUILDINGS, OVER
STREETS, OVER THE PATH OF THE WINDING RIVER.
THE LANDSCAPE BLURRED -
IN A BLINK OF A MOMENT -
WE WERE UPON A MOUNTAIN OF SAND!
ALL AROUND US, IT WAS BLACKNESS!
YET -
IN THE BLACKNESS -
THERE WAS SHADOWY FORMS!

MY JESUS GLOWED AS A BLAZING TORCH -
WHERE HIS LIGHT SHONE -
THE SHADOWY FORMS IN A RASPY WHINING SCREECH
CRAWLED BACK INTO THE BLACKNESS -
FOR THE LIGHT JESUS SHONE -
THE. LIGHT THAT BLAZED DEEPLY WITHIN HIM -
THAT LIGHT THAT GLOWED AS A NOONDAY SUN -
BLINDED THESE SHADOWY CITIZENS OF THIS
STRANGE LAND.

IN A SMALL TREMBLING VOICE, I SPOKE:
"PRECIOUS JESUS OF NAZARETH -
"WHO ARE THESE STRANGE BEINGS?"
"WHERE ARE WE?"
IN A VOICE THAT SPOKE OF FOAMY SEA WATERS -
HE SPOKE TO HIS SERVANT -
"BELOVED -
"FEAR NOT!"
FOR THIS IS MY LESSON I SHALL WRITE UPON YOUR
HEART!"
"WE ARE IN THE WASTELAND!"
"THESE ARE THE LOST SOULS WHO ROAM THIS DESO-
LATE LAND."

"ONCE THERE WAS PEACE AND PROSPERITY,
"SEE MY ENEMY HAS PLUNDERED MY GRACE!"
WITH A TROUBLED HEART, I SPOKE TO MY BELOVED
LORD:
"LORD -
"FORGIVE YOUR SERVANT!"
"I DO NOT UNDERSTAND!"
"PLEASE, LORD, I NEED YOUR WISDOM!"

"LOOK AROUND YOU, MY BELOVED!"
"THIS WAS MY GARDEN IN WHOM WE DELIGHTED IN!"
"SEE HOW MY ENEMY WON ENTRANCE -
"WITH LIES AND DECEPTION, HE TORE DOWN THE
BEAUTIFUL GATES OF ZION!"
"YES, THERE WERE MY FEW FAITHFUL SERVANTS WHO
VALIANTLY FOUGHT THE BATTLE -
"BUT, GREAT WAS THE WILL OF THE CITIZENS WITHIN
THIS CITY -
"FOR THEY WERE DECEIVED AND SEDUCED BY THE
ENEMY!"
"AND AS THE THIEF WHICH IS HIS TRUE NATURE,
"ALONG WITH HIS DARK FALLEN COMPANIONS,
"SWARMED IN LUSTFUL GLEE, THE LOCUSTS
SWARMED UPON THE GOLDEN FIELDS OF WHEAT!"
"ALAS!"
THEY CAME AND RAVAGED EVERY LIVING THING -
"LEAVING DESOLATION AND A WASTELAND!"
"FAMINE HAS FALLEN UPON THEM!"
"THEIR LAMENTATIONS FILL THE FIRMAMENT -
"YET -
"THEY KNOW ME NOT!"
"GONE IS THE GRACE OF MY HOLY WILL!"
"GONE IS THE BROKEN MANNA, MY FAITHFUL SER-
VANTS SERVED TO THE LOST AND WOUNDED SOULS
THE ENEMY HAS LAID WASTE TO!"
"GONE IS THE BREATH OF SALVATION -

"FOR THEY HAVE GRIEVED MY HOLY SPIRIT AWAY!
"YET -
"FOR THE SAKE OF THE ELECT REMNANT -
"MY ARMS ARE STILL WELCOMING MY LOST CHIL-
DREN -
"AS THE FATHER, WITH JOY WELCOME THE RETURN OF
HIS BELOVED PRODIGAL SON!"
"EVEN IN THE DARKNESS, EVEN IN THE DESOLATION, I
CALL MY CHOSEN -
"COME!"
"FOLLOW ME!"
"I AM THE ONLY TRUE LIGHT OF LIFE!"
"I AM THE ONLY TRUE WAY TO LIFE EVERLASTING!"
"I AM THE ONLY TRUE DOOR OF YOUR HOPE!"
"I AM THE ONLY TRUTH!"
"I AM THE ONLY WAY TO BRING YOU INTO MY
FATHER'S KINGDOM!"
"YET, THEY MOCKED ME, ONCE AGAIN!"
"YET, THEY SCORNED ME, ONCE AGAIN!"
"YET, THEY CRIED OUT ONCE AGAIN - 'CRUCIFY HIM!

IN THE VINEYARDS, I'VE SENT MY BELOVED SER-
VANTS, THEY LABORED FAITHFULLY, SOME PREPARED
THE GROUND, SOME SOWED THE SEEDS, SOME TORE
THE CHOKING WEEDS THAT SPRUNG AROUND THE
ROOTS, SOME WITH THE GUIDANCE OF MY HOLY SPIR-
IT DID THE PRUNING EVER SO GENTLY AS TO NOT
DAMAGE OR DESTROY THE YOUNG VINELINGS! STILL
SOME GATHERED THE GRAPES, AND AGAIN BY MY
HOLY SPIRIT WERE PRESSED TILL THE NEW WINE WAS
MADE!

" SEE -
"HOW WHITE AS SNOW IS THE HARVEST?
"HOW MY FAITHFUL SERVANTS TOILED TO GATHER
THE HARVEST IN BEFORE THE PLAGUE OF DESOLA-

TION WOULD BE UPON THEM!

"HOW GREEDILY THE LOCUST EYED THE HARVEST -

"WAITING FOR THE APPOINTED TIME TO DEVOUR ALL LIFE -

"LEAVING DEATH BEHIND THEIR ANGRY LUSTFUL WAKE -

"LEAVING SICKNESS BEHIND THEIR MOCKING LAUGHTER -

"LEAVING FAMINE BEHIND FOR THE CITIZENS MEAGERLY IF AT ALL PARTOOK OF THE WEALTH OF THE LAND!

"LEAVING DESOLATION BEHIND FOR THE CITIZENS HAVE GROWN FATTED UPON THEIR OWN ACQUIRED WEALTH!"

"DO YOU NOT SEE, MY BELOVED!"

"MY PEOPLE CHOSE TO FOLLOW THEIR CARNAL "gods",

"THEY HAVE ALLOWED STRANGE IDOLS TO COME INTO THEIR HOUSEHOLDS -

"THEY HAVE GIVEN SACRIFICE TO THESE FALSE "gods"!"

"GREATLY THEY HAVE FANNED MY ANGER AGAINST THESE STIFF-NECKED PEOPLE!

"NOW -

"NOT EVEN THE BIRDS WILL FEED UPON THEIR MAGGOT FILLED CORPSES!

"FOR THEY HAVE BROUGHT UPON THEMSELVES THE JUDGMENT OF GOMORRAH!

"NOW THEY SCURRY AWAY FROM MY GLORY -

"FOR GREAT IS THEIR APOSTASY!"

"FOR GREAT ARE THEIR ABOMINATIONS IN MY SIGHT!

"NOW, THEY SHALL EAT OF THE DUST!

"FOR MY WORDS WERE LIFE UNTO THEM!

"TOGETHER WE WALKED IN THE GARDEN -

"WE WERE ONE!"

"NOW, MY ENEMIES HAVE DECEIVED AND SEDUCED MY PEOPLE -
"MY SERVANTS, WHO PROFESSED THEIR LOVE PRO-FUSELY -
"NOW, HAVE SET THEMSELVES AGAINST MY WILL!"
"COME, BELOVED!"

HERE I AM SITTING UPON MY BED -
I WALK TO MY WINDOW -
AND I DO NOT SEE THE GREENERY -
THE VERDANT LIFE OF ABBA FATHER!
BUT NOW, I SEE WITH MY FATHER'S EYES -
THE LOCUST HAS COME -
QUICKLY THEY ARE DEVOURING THE LIFE-GIVING WORDS THAT JESUS OF NAZARETH SPOKE TO HIS DIS-CIPLES WHEN HE WALKED AMONG US!
TEARS STREAMED DOWN MY CHEEKS, I COULD SEE THE MOLTEN SILVERY TEARS OF MY SWEET LORD, WITH ALL OF MY HEART I SPOKE"
"LORD!"
"END THIS TERRIBLE DEVASTATION!"
"RESTORE YOUR GRACE AND MERCY UPON US!"
SADLY, HE SMILED A TENDER SMILE -
"MY BELOVED, SPEAK OF THESE THINGS TO ALL I BRING ACROSS YOUR PATH -
"THOSE WHO WILL ACCEPT ME -
"THEY SHALL BE GIVEN GRACE AND MERCY -
"BUT WOE UNTO THOSE WHO REFUSE!
"FOR GREAT WILL BE MY WRATH UPON THEM!"

"I AM THE LORD, I AM ONE!"
"THERE IS NOT OTHER!"
"FOR I AM YOUR ALPHA -
"I AM YOUR OMEGA -
"I AM THE WAY TO EVERLASTING LIFE!
"I AM THE TRUTH TO SPEAK THROUGH YOU MY

FATHER'S WORDS OF LIFE!
"KEEP THEM ALWAYS ON YOUR LIPS -
"WITH PRAISE AND THANKSGIVING -
"LET US BE ONE IN WILL, BELOVED -
"LET US BE ONE IN PURPOSE, BELOVED -
"LET US BRING THE LOST HOME,
"LET US BRING THE BLIND SO THAT THEY MAY SEE
THE KINGDOM IS AT HAND!
"LET US HEAL AND ANOINT THE BROKEN-HEARTED,
"THOSE WHO HAVE BEEN SORELY AFFLICTED BY THE
POISONOUS BITES OF THE LOCUST -
"LET US CAST OUT THE ENEMY FROM MY HOLY
MOUNT -
"FOR IN MY NAME, GREATER THINGS YOU SHALL DO!"

"SO, MY BELOVED -
"STAND FIRM ON THE VICTORY OF CALVARY!
"SPEAK OF THIS VISION TO MY PEOPLE -
"SO THAT THEY WILL SEE WITH THEIR HEAVENLY
FATHER'S EYES -
"NOT THAT DARK VISION OF OUR ENEMY!
"MY ENEMY'S SIGHT IS DEATH, FAMINE, DESTRUCTION -
MY VISION IS OF EVERLASTING LIFE FOREVER IN THE
GLORY AND PRESENCE OF ABBA FATHER -
"FOR BY MY ATONING SACRIFICE -
"I WILLINGLY LAID DOWN MY LIFE -
SO THAT TOGETHER WE WILL RISE TO A NEW DAWN OF
HOPE AND VICTORY!

(*Footnote)
Praise the Lord! Received and "experienced" this on 6/20/94 at
10:20 P.M. Finished this at 11:36 P.M.

GETHSEMANE
BY THE HOLY SPIRIT

MY BELOVED -
COME!
FEAR NOT!
THOUGH IT BE MIDNIGHT -
DAWN IS QUICKLY APPROACHING!
IS MY LIGHT AT THE WINDOW OF YOUR SOUL?
HAVE YOU THE ANOINTED OIL OF MY HOLY SPIRIT?
SEE -
I AM COMING, MY BELOVED -
HOLD FAST!
FOR THOUGH THE ENEMY IS FIERCE,
AND THE STORMS OF LIFE ARE BLOWING FURIOUSLY
AT YOU -
FEAR NOT!
DO NOT DESPAIR!
DO NOT SEEK ANY OTHER WAYS TO AVOID THE
STORM!
THERE IS NO OTHER WAY, BUT BY ME!
I AM THE ONLY LIGHT AND THE ONLY WAY IN THIS
HOUR OF YOUR GETHSEMANE!
YES, BELOVED -
AS MY BRIDE -
YOU TOO, MUST DECIDE, AS I DECIDED, THAT I WILL
DO MY FATHER'S WILL, NOT MINE!
AS MY BRIDE -
YOU, TOO, WILL BE DELIVERED TO THE HIGH PRIEST
OF THE SYNAGOGUE -
AND THE WHIPS OF HATRED WILL STRIKE YOU!

DO NOT CRY OUT BELOVED -
BUT LET YOUR SPIRIT RISE AND REJOICE -
SING PRAISES TO YOUR ABBA FATHER -
FOR ALL WHO ARE IN DARKNESS WILL SEE HIS GLORY
THROUGH YOU!
YES, BELOVED, REJOICE!
FOR AS THE WORLD HATED AND PERSECUTED ME -
THEY WITH ALL THE FURY OF HELL WILL ALSO DO
UNTO YOU!
SO, MY BELOVED BRIDE -
FEAR NOT!
AS I LAID MY LIFE WILLINGLY DOWN FOR YOU TO
HAVE EVERLASTING LIFE NOW COMES THE TIME OF
LAMENTATION!
AS RACHEL CRIED FOR HER MURDERED CHILDREN -
CRY ALSO, MY BELOVED, FOR THE SAINTS WHO WILL
BE MARTYRED FOR MY SAKE!
IT IS TIME, MY BELOVED, THAT I AM ASKING YOU TO
WILLINGLY LAY DOWN YOUR LIFE, SO THE LOST AND
WOUNDED CHILDREN MAY BE RELEASED FROM THE
DUNGEONS OF OUR ENEMY!
COME, MY BELOVED BRIDE -
LET US GATHER THE SHEEP INTO OUR FOLD,
LET THE GOATS BE HERDED FOR SLAUGHTER,
FOR THE GOATS ARE THE CHILDREN OF DARKNESS -
SOON THEY WILL SHARE THE SAME FATE AS THEIR
FATHER -
THEY WILL ALL BE THROWN IN THE LAKE OF FIRE!
COME, MY BELOVED, THERE IS JUST A FEW PRECIOUS
MOMENTS OF LABOR BEFORE THE ANGELS SOUND
THEIR TRUMPETS -
ANNOUNCING TO THE WORLD THAT JEHOVAH'S WINE-
PRESS OF WRATH IS FILLED TO OVERFLOWING!

MY BELOVED -
BEWARE OF FALSE PROPHETS WHO PROPHECY IN MY
NAME A TIME OF PEACE AND CONTENTMENT -
BEWARE -
WAR WILL BE AT YOUR DOORSTEP!

BELOVED -
PREPARE MY LOST REMNANT THAT THEIR MESSIAH IS
FAST APPROACHING -
AND MY HEAVENLY HOSTS ARE EVEN AT THIS
MOMENT GATHERING MY PEOPLE FROM THE FOUR
CORNERS OF THE EARTH!
IT IS NOW TIME TO BEGIN THE MARRIAGE FEAST!
THOSE WHO HEAR THE INVITATION -
SHALL BE GIVEN NEW GARMENTS OF FINE PURE
LINEN -
THEY SHALL BE CLEANSED AND MADE WHOLE -
THEY SHALL RECEIVE THEIR CROWNS OF LIFE!
THOSE WHO REFUSE MY INVITATION -
THOSE WHO RATHER FEAST WITH THE ENEMY -
SHALL FOREVER BE CAST IN THEIR DARKNESS -
THEY SHALL GNASH THEIR TEETH WITH THE FURY OF
THOSE WHOM THEY FEASTED -
GREAT WILL BE THEIR EVERLASTING TORMENT!
SO, COME, MY BELOVED BRIDE,
THE WATCHMAN'S TRUMPET IS SOUNDING -
MIDNIGHT IS UPON THEE -
BUT -
FEAR NOT!
FOR I WILL ALWAYS BE WITH THEE -
NO WEAPONS FORMED AGAINST THEE SHALL PREVAIL -
THE GATES OF HELL ALSO SHALL NOT PREVAIL
AGAINST THEE!
SO, MY BELOVED BRIDE,
COME SINGING PRAISES -
COME DANCING WITH JOY -

FOR I YOUR BRIDEGROOM -
NOW CLAIMS HIS BRIDE FOR HIS GLORY!

(*Footnote)
Amen! Praise the Lord! Started this Saturday, Jan. 29, 1994 at
12:00 P.M. while being a patient in the hospital and finished this
at 12:20 P.M. Hallelujah! Glory to the Lord forever!
Amen! Amen!

THE BLESSED ANTICIPATION
OF PROMISES KEPT

THE BLACKSMITH AND THE SWORD

IN THE PRE-DAWN MISTS OF TIME -
A BLACKSMITH WENT INTO THE DEEP CAVERNS OF
HADES -
THERE HE METICULOUSLY CHOSE A LUMP OF BLACK-
ENED STONE. IN HIS TORCHLIGHT, GLINTS REFLECTED
FROM THE LIFELESS LUMP. WITH A SECRET SMILE OF
SATISFACTION -
HE LEFT THE CAVERNS OF SILENT BLACKNESS -
HE RETURNED TO HIS FORGERY.

IN THE PRE-DAWN MISTS OF TIME -
THE BLACKSMITH WITH HIS TOOLS TOILED OVER A
LUMP OF BLACKENED STONE.
IN THE FORGERY -
THE CRACKLING OF THE BLACKSMITH'S FIRE BLAZED
FURIOUSLY!
IN A BARREL OF THE FINEST CEDAR WOOD IT WAS
FILLED WITH CRYSTAL CLEAR WATER FROM THE
MOUNTAIN PEAK GAVE OFF IT'S STEAM IN THE
INTENSE HEAT OF THE HAMMERED BLACKENED
LUMP!
NOW THE BLACKSMITH IN THE FULL GLORY OF THE
DAY -
CAREFULLY CHIPPED AT THE LIFELESS LUMP OF
BLACKNESS -
DROPS OF SWEAT TRICKLED DOWN UPON IT AS KISSES
OF THE BLACKSMITH'S LIFE -
LOVINGLY HE FASHIONED THE BLACKENED LUMP
INTO A CRUDE BLADE -
HE SIGHS WITH A LABORIOUS BREATHS UPON IT,

INFUSING HIS LIE AND WILL INTO THE CRUDE BLADE!
HIS VOICE THUNDERS IN EXALTATION!
"YOU, MY BELOVED, SHALL BE MY PERFECT WEAPON
AGAINST MY ENEMY AND HIS FALSE KINGDOM!"
"YOU, MY BELOVED, SHALL BRING FORTH MY
ENSLAVED CHILDREN TO VICTORY AND FREEDOM!"
"TOGETHER, MY BELOVED, WE SHALL CONQUER ALL
THOSE WHO ARE AGAINST ME!

ALL DURING THE DAY -
THE BLACKSMITH LABORED -
SIX DAYS HE CHIPPED AND FASHIONED HIS BLADE
FROM THE LIFELESS CRUDE SHAPED BLADE OF
BLACKENED STONE!
ON THE SEVENTH DAY -
SEEING HIS WORK WAS GOOD -
THE BLACKSMITH RESTED FROM HIS LOVING CRE-
ATION!

ONE STORMY DAY -
THE BLACKSMITH WITH RAGE AND FURY -
CAME TO HIS FORGERY -
HE STOKED HIS FIRE OF WRATH -
WITH HIS BREATH, HE COOLED THE MOUNTAIN-TOP
WATER -
THERE UPON HIS TABLE -
WITH A THUNDEROUS VOICE, HE BELLOWS:
"MY ENEMY HAS KILLED MY ONE AND ONLY BELOVED
SON!"
"DAILY HE FEEDS UPON THE BLOOD OF MY CHIL-
DREN!"
"I'VE SENT MY ONLY CHILD TO RESCUE MY LOST CHIL-
DREN -
"HE SO LOVINGLY OBEYED MY WILL AND OFFERED HIS
LIFE AS THE RANSOM PRICE OF FREEDOM -
"HE SEARCHED THE EARTH FOR MY CHILDREN -

"AS HE FOUND THEM, HE HEALED THEM FROM MY ENEMIES ATTACK -
"HE TAUGHT THEM THE TRUTH THAT I AM REALLY THEIR TRUE FATHER -
"I HAVE CREATED THEM FOR MY GOOD PLEASURE -
"I ONLY WANT THEIR LOVE IN RETURN!"
"BUT MY ADVERSARY BLINDED MY FOOLISH CHILDREN WITH A SILKEN TONGUE OF DECEPTION -
"WITH GOLDEN PROMISES OF WEALTH AND GRANDEUR AND POWER -
"HE RECRUITED THEM AS A PIPER LURES HIS VICTIMS TO THEIR DEATHS!
"MY ADVERSARY HAS TURNED MY CHILDREN AGAINST MY ONLY SON AND VICIOUSLY TORE AT HIS INNOCENT BODY!"
"HOW THEY MOCKED AND SHAMED HIM PUBLICLY!
"THEN THEY HUNG MY BELOVED SON UPON A CROSS MADE OF ROUGH HEWN WOOD!
"NOW I SHALL VINDICATE MYSELF UPON MY ENEMIES!"
"THOSE WHO RECEIVE MY SON AS THEIR LORD AND SAVIOR -
"THOSE WHO COME TO ME THROUGH HIS SACRIFICE OF LOVE -
"REPENTING TO ME IN HIS NAME -
"I WILL TAKE THEM OUT OF THE CAVERNS OF DEATH -
"AND I SHALL FORGE THEM AS I HAVE CREATED THIS BLADE -
"THEY SHALL BE GLORIOUS SWORDS OF MY HOLY SPIRIT!"
"MY ENEMIES WILL COWER IN THE FEAR OF ME!"

IN THE STORMY NIGHT OF TIME -
THE BLACKSMITH LABORED UPON THE CRUDE BLACK BLADE HE GAVE THE BLADE HIS BREATH OF LIFE -
IN A TREMBLING SMALL VOICE THE BLADE FIRST

SPOKE:

"MY LORD, WHAT IS YOUR PURPOSE FOR ME?"

IN A VOICE THAT SOUNDED LIKE A MIGHTY RUSHING WATERS -

THE BLACKSMITH SPOKE:

"MY ONLY BEGOTTEN SON WAS GIVEN AS A RANSOM TO MY ENEMY SO THAT MY CHILDREN CAN BE SET FREE FROM HIS DARK, VILE KINGDOM OF DEATH!"

"I HAVE SET MY WILL UPON YOU, LITTLE ONE -

"I NOW NEED TO HAVE A MIGHTY WEAPON TO AVENGE MY WRATH AGAINST MY ADVERSARY -

"WILL YOU BE MY SWORD OF MY SPIRIT, AS MY SON'S BLADE OF VICTORY?"

"WILL YOU SERVE MY SON AS YOUR KING?"

EXCITEDLY, THE CRUDE BLACK BLADE REPLIED:

"OH! YES! MY LORD AND MASTER!"

"I WILL BE HONORED TO SERVE YOU!"

IN A SOFT VOICE, THE BLACKSMITH SPOKE TO HIS CRUDE BLACK BLADE:

"MY LITTLE ONE, THERE IS A PRICE YOU MUST PAY -

"JUST AS MY SON PAID THE PRICE BY WILLINGLY LAYING DOWN HIS LIFE -

"SO MUST YOU, MY BELOVED CHILD!"

"ARE YOU WILLING TO LAY DOWN YOUR WILL AND ALLOW ME TO FASHION YOU AS I SEE FIT?"

"OH! YES! MASTER, LET YOUR WILL BE DONE UPON ME!"

JOYFULLY THE NEW BLADE CRIED OUT!

WITH GREAT DELIGHT, THE BLACKSMITH BEGAN HIS LABOR OF LOVE -

TO FASHION A MIGHTY PERFECT SWORD FOR HIS BELOVED SON!

SO WITH THE IRON HAMMER OF HIS WILL, HE BEGAN TO SOFTEN THE CRUDE BLADE -

"OUCH! STOP IT! CRIED THE BLACKISH-GRAY SWORD.

"YOU'RE HURTING ME!"

IN A SOFT WHISPER, THE BLACKSMITH SMOOTHED
THE CHIPS OF BLACK OFF THE BLADE -

DROPS OF SWEAT FROM HIS BROW FELL UPON THE
BATTERED BLADE -

"OH! MY LITTLE ONE, THIS IS THE PRICE I SPOKE TO
YOU THAT YOU MUST PAY TO BE MY MIGHTY SWORD!"

IN A BRASH, ARROGANT VOICE, THE BLADE SPOKE:

"I AM A FINE SWORD NOW!"

"I CAN FELL YOUR ENEMIES IN A BLOW!"

"CAN YOU, NOW, MY FOOLISH LITTLE BLADE!" THE
BLACKSMITH ROARED IN A LAUGHING TONE.

THE LITTLE BLADE BECAME QUITE OFFENDED BY HIS
MASTER'S TOM-FOOLERY!

"YES, MY LORD! I CAN GIVE QUITE A BITE TO YOUR
NASTY ENEMIES!"

"SO, PLEASE DO NOT HAMMER AT ME ANY MORE!"

IN A KINGLY AUTHORITATIVE VOICE, THE BLACK-
SMITH SPOKE:

'LITTLE ONE, AS YOU ARE NOW, ONE MIGHTY BLOW
FROM MY ENEMY'S DARK VENOM FILLED SWORD AND
YOU WILL DIE!"

THE LITTLE BLADE BARTERED WITH HIS MASTER
CEASELESSLY -

WITH A SIGH OF RESIGNATION, THE BLACKSMITH
WENT TO HIS SON.

"MY BELOVED SON, THIS LITTLE BLADE INSISTS IT IS
READY FOR YOUR PURPOSE AGAINST THE ENEMY -

"PLEASE TEST THIS BLADE, SEE IF IT IS TO YOUR SAT-
ISFACTION."

"YES, FATHER!" REPLIED THE HANDSOME YOUNG SON.

SO OUT TO BATTLE THEY SET OUT -

IN A BUBBLY BROOK VOICE, THE SON SPOKE TO THE
LITTLE BLADE -

"SO, MY LITTLE ONE!"

"YOU ARE SO FILLED WITH CERTAINTY THAT YOU
WILL BE VICTORIOUS AGAINST MY ENEMY?"

"OH! YES! MY LORD! I WILL GIVE YOU A GLORIOUS VICTORY AGAINST YOUR ENEMY AND ALL YOUR CHILDREN WILL BE SET FREE!"
REPLIED THE CONFIDENT GRAY-BLACK SPECKLED BLADE.

IN THE GRAY CLOUDED, STORMY DAY OF THE BATTLE - THE ENEMY SAW THE CRUDE GRAY SPECKLED LITTLE BLADE -
HE CROWED IN GLEEFUL JOY!
"OH! MY KING! IS THIS YOUR GREAT AND MIGHTY SWORD?"
"SHOULD I COWER IN SHAMEFUL DEFEAT?" NOT THIS DAY, MY LORD!"
"FOR I WILL DESTROY THIS FOOLISH BLADE!"
IN A MIGHTY RUSH, THE TWO LORDS -
ONE IN BRIGHT GOLDEN ARMOR,
THE OTHER IN MIDNIGHT BLACKNESS -
BLADES THRUST AT ONE ANOTHER -
THE LITTLE BLADE, TOO LATE, SAW IT'S FOOLHARDINESS OF CONFIDENT PROWESS -
IN TOTAL HUMILITY, THE DARK LORD GAVE IT'S LASH OF DEFEAT!

IN THE STILLNESS OF THE NIGHT -
THE BLACKSMITH AND HIS SON WHISPERED IN THE SHADOWS OF TIME -
THIS LITTLE BLADE HAS LEARNED IT'S FIRST LESSON OF DEFEAT!
AGAINST THE MASTER'S BEST INTENTIONS -
THE LITTLE BLADE INSISTED IT'S OWN WILL TO BE DONE!
NOW, THE LITTLE BLADE CRIED SORROWFULLY -
"FORGIVE ME, MY FATHER!"
"FORGIVE ME, MY LORD!"
"THE ARDOR OF MY NEW FORM, FILLED ME WITH A

PASSION THAT I COULD CONQUER ANYONE!"

IN A SILKEN VOICE OF COMPASSION THEY SPOKE AS ONE:

"LITTLE ONE -

"THE COST OF BECOMING A MIGHTY SWORD IS GREAT -

"ARE YOU WILLING TO LET US MOLD YOU AS WE DESIRE?"

"OR ARE YOU SO BENT UPON YOUR OWN WILL AND GLORY?"

"FOR IF YOU ARE SO AGAINST US -

"THEN WE WILL HAVE TO PUT YOU BACK IN THE DARK SILENT CAVERNS OF HADES -

"AND CHOOSE ANOTHER WHO WILL BE ONE IN OUR DESIGN AND PURPOSE AGAINST OUR ENEMY IN THIS THE LAST FINAL BATTLE!"

"OH! NO! MY LORD! MASTER, I AM WILLING TO PAY THE COST, NO MATTER WHAT IT IS!"

"I WANT TO DO YOUR WILL, CERTAINLY AFTER THIS TASTE OF BATTLE WITH THE ENEMY -

"I MUST DO AS YOU DEEM NECESSARY OF ME!"

WITH A SIGH OF DEEP PATIENCE, THE BLACKSMITH, BEGAN HIS LABOR OF LOVE ONCE AGAIN!

ONCE AGAIN, THE BLACKSMITH HAMMERED AND CHISELED AND FASHIONED THE CRUDE LITTLE GRAY-SPECKLED BLADE -

STOICALLY, THE BRAVE LITTLE BLADE SURRENDERED ITSELF TO THE MASTER'S WILL!

THEN, ONE DAY -

THE BLACKSMITH SPOKE TO THE FIERY FURNACE -

THE BLACKSMITH SPOKE TO THE COOL MOUNTAIN-TOP WATER -

"ARE YOU WILLING TO BE A PART OF MY NEW BLADE TO WIELD AGAINST OUR ENEMIES?"

"YES" THEY REPLIED AS ONE -

"FOR WE ARE YOUR SPIRIT, MELD OUR ELEMENTS TO

THY WILL!"

SO THE BLACKSMITH, TOOK THE LITTLE BLADE AND PUT IT THROUGH THE FIERY FURNACE -

THEN QUICKLY COOLED THE MOLTEN MOLD OF HIS SWORD INTO THE MOUNTAIN-TOP WATER -

THE LITTLE SWORD TREMBLED AT THE EXPERIENCE OF THIS NEW TEST -

"MASTER, HOW LONG WILL YOU SMITE ME?"

"I CANNOT BEAR IT ANY LONGER!"

"SPARE ME, MY LORD! OR I SHALL SURELY DIE!"

"NOT AT THE HAND OF YOUR ENEMY -

"BUT AT YOUR HAND AND YOUR MERCILESS WILL!"

THE BLACKSMITH SIGHED WITH TEMPERANCE UPON HIS NEW SWORD -

"LITTLE ONE, I MUST NOW FORGE YOU TO THE HANDLE OF MY WILL AND PURPOSE -

"I WILL NOT SLAY YOU, MY BELOVED, FOR YOU ARE NOW AS ONE OF MY BELOVED CHILDREN!"

"I WILL NOT ABANDON YOU, NOR FORSAKE YOU, AS YOU GO THROUGH THESE TRIALS -

"TRUST ME, LITTLE ONE!"

THE LITTLE DULL GRAY BLADE SIGHED WITH A SHUDDERING BREATH -

"MY LORD, LET YOUR WILL BE MY WILL!"

AND SO THE BLACKSMITH, ONCE AGAIN, IN LOVING LABOR, ROLLED UP HIS SLEEVE AND BEGAN TO STRETCH THE BLADE TILL IT COULD NOT BE STRETCHED ANYMORE.

IN BATH OF FIRE, IN BATH OF COOL REFRESHING WATER, WITH HAMMER, THE BLACKSMITH WORKED THRU THE DAY!

HE HAD TO HAVE HIS SWORD FINISHED BY THE MIDNIGHT HOUR -

FOR THEN THE FINAL BATTLE WILL BE FOUGHT!

HIS ENEMY, HE WILL VINDICATE FOR THE MANY HORRIBLE ABOMINATIONS HE COMMITTED AGAINST HIM,

AGAINST HIS BELOVED SON, AGAINST HIS CHOSEN
CHILDREN.
ALL THROUGH THE TESTING, STRETCHING AND TEM-
PERING OF HIS MIGHTY BLADE -
THE BLADE IN SILENT TEARS FLOWING -
A DEEP SILVERY GLOW BEGAN TO RISE FROM WITHIN -
THE BLACKSMITH BEGAN TO REJOICE!
ALL HIS LABOR WAS NOT IN VAIN!
FOR THE LITTLE SWORD WITHSTOOD ALL OF THE
MOLDING AND TESTING AND THE GLINTS HE CAUGHT
WITHIN THAT BLACKENED LUMP HE FOUND IN THE
CAVES OF HADES WAS BEGINNING TO EMERGE TO THE
SURFACE A HIGH SILVERY SHEEN!
"NOW I WILL WIELD YOU TO MY WILL, AND AS ONE WE
WILL DEFEAT OUR FOE!"
THE BLACKSMITH PRESENTED THIS BEAUTIFUL MAG-
NIFICENT SWORD TO HIS BELOVED SON -
IN WONDROUS AWE AND JOY THE SON REJOICED WITH
HIS FATHER!
HE SWUNG HIS NEW WEAPON -
A SONG SPRANG FROM THE HEART OF THE BLADE -
A SONG OF VICTORY!
THE MIRROR SHARP SWORD SANG WITH HER LORD!
HER HILT WAS FASHIONED WITH PRECIOUS STONES AND
PEARLS FORMED FROM THE LITTLE BLADE'S TEARS!
WHAT A MARVELOUS WEAPON IT HAD BECOME!

IN THE MIDNIGHT HOUR -
THE LORD CAME AS A THIEF IN THE NIGHT -
HE CALLED HIS BRIDE -
AND TO HIS BELOVED -
HE PRESENTED HER HIS MIGHTY SWORD -
"JUSTICE/REAPER" WAS THE NAME OF HIS SWORD -
FOR HIS FATHER, THE BLACKSMITH, HAD GIVEN HIM A
DOUBLE-EDGED SWORD.
FOR THIS SWORD WOULD REAP HIS RIGHTFUL GOLD-

EN INHERITANCE -

AND THEN HE WOULD WIELD HIS JUSTICE ON THE ENEMY THAT ENSLAVED, TORMENTED HIS FATHER'S BELOVED CHILDREN!

SO MY FRIEND -
WE MUST BE LIKE THAT LITTLE LUMP OF BLACKNESS -
FOR WE WERE IN THE PITS OF DEATH -
ABBA FATHER - THE BLACKSMITH KNOWING OUR INNER BEING -
CHOSE US AND OUT OF THE BLACKNESS HE FASHIONED US TO BE HIS WEAPON AGAINST OUR ENEMY - satan!
SO WHEN YOU FEEL THE HAMMERING -
REJOICE!
WHEN YOU FEEL THE HOT BREATH OF THE FIERY FURNACE -
PERSEVERE!
WHEN YOU FEEL THE COOLNESS OF THE LIVING MOUNTAIN-TOP WATER -
REST IN THE LORD THY GOD!
AND THROUGH ALL THIS - LET YOUR TEARS BE FOR ALL THE CHILDREN -
THE BRIDE OF THE BELOVED -
BECAUSE THE LORD IS IN NEED OF A MIGHTY SWORD OF HIS HOLY SPIRIT -
TO VANQUISH FOREVER HIS ADVERSARY AND TO SET HIS PEOPLE FREE -
AND TO BRING THEM TO THEIR RIGHTFUL HOME -
THE LORD'S KINGDOM OF LOVE!

(*Footnote)
Praise the Lord! Tonight I picked up the unfinished story of the Blacksmith I started this on 2/5/94 at 10:00 A.M. Finished this on 9/15/96 at 12:02 A.M.

PROPHECY 4/10/92

MY BELOVED CHILDREN!
NOW IS THE TIME TO COME OUT OF THE BELLY OF THE WHALE!
COME OUT OF THE TOMBS!
COME AWAKE FROM YOUR SLUMBER!
COME UNTO ME!
IT IS TIME TO PUT ON THE GARMENTS OF WARFARE!
FOR IT IS TIME TO GATHER THE WOUNDED, THE DYING!
STAND FIRM IN PRAYER AND SUPPLICATION FOR THESE LOST SOULS TILL MY ANGELS BRING THEM INTO MY SANCTUARY!
FOR THIS IS THE TIME OF HEALING AND RESTORATION, AND MY HOLY SPIRIT TO BE THE GENERAL OF HE BATTLE!
NOW IT IS TIME FOR THE SHEEP TO COME TO ME -
TIME IS COMING TO A COMPLETION!
I AM AT THE DOOR OF YOUR HEART, KNOCKING -
THOSE WHO WILL WELCOME ME -
I WILL BLESS -
THOSE WHO KNOW ME NOT -
I SHALL NOT ACKNOWLEDGE THEM AT THE WEDDING FEAST!
SO COME!
PUT ON YOUR ROBES OF AUTHORITY THAT I'VE GIVEN TO YOU!
THE HARVEST IS RIPE, IT IS TIME FOR THE GATHERING -
FOR SOON, I WILL BE AMONG THOSE WHOM I'VE PREPARED AND CALLED -
AND TOGETHER, MY HOUSE WILL BE RESTORED TO

200

THE GLORY OF MY FATHER!
NO LONGER WILL MY HOUSE BE A DEN OF THIEVES
AND MONEY-CHANGERS!
SO COME!
PUT ON YOUR GARMENTS OF PRAISE -
PUT ON YOUR GARMENTS OF CRIMSON -
PUT ON YOUR GARMENTS OF SALVATION -
FOR I STRETCH FORTH MY HAND TO MY BELOVED
BRIDE!

FAREWELL TO A BELOVED FRIEND!

IN THE PASSAGE OF TIME -
WE COME ACROSS SO MANY STRANGERS -
YET -
OUT OF THE SEA -
THERE'S AN OYSTER WITH A PRECIOUS PEARL -
SO TOO, WHEN OUT OF THE CROWD -
A PRECIOUS FRIEND IS FOUND!

MEMORIES WEAVE A FABRIC WOVEN WITH LAUGH-
TER, WITH TEARS AND WITH LOVE!
OH! MY BELOVED FRIEND -
THE MEMORIES YOU HAVE WOVEN IN MY SHORT TIME
KNOWING YOU -
WILL EVER BE WITH ME!

HOW WE TAKE TIME FOR GRANTED!
HOW WE PUT OFF LIVING PRECIOUS MOMENTS WITH
OUR LOVED ONES!
FOR THERE'S ALWAYS A TOMORROW TO HAVE A CHAT!
FOR THERE'S ALWAYS A TOMORROW TO HAVE SOME
TIME TOGETHER TO SHARE -
YET -
HERE'S TOMORROW!
FOR YOU HAVE SLIPPED AWAY!
IT WAS YOUR TIME TO REST AND GO HOME TO THE
LORD!
NOW YOU ARE WITH THE EVERLASTING FAITHFUL
FRIEND -
MUCH MORE THAN I CAN EVER CLAIM -

YET - TEARS OF GRIEF FLOW FREELY DOWN MY CHEEKS AND ALL MY "IFS" COME HAUNTING ME!

SO NOW IN THE BRIEF PASSAGE OF TIME WE SHARED - HOW CAN I EVER TELL YOU HOW MUCH I CHERISHED YOUR FRIENDSHIP!
HOW CAN I EVER TELL YOU HOW THANKFUL TO THE DEAR LORD I AM FOR ALLOWING ME TO SHARE A TINY FRACTION OF MY LIFE WITH ONE WHO SHARED IN MY JOYS,
WITH ONE WHO SHARED IN MY TRIALS,
WITH ONE WHO NEVER FAILED TO SHOW HOPE!

SO HERE I SIT - PENNING THIS FAREWELL - TEARS FLOWING FROM A GRIEF OF NEVER HAVING TOLD YOU: "THANK YOU FOR BEING MY FRIEND!"

YET -
AS YOU NOW ABIDE WITH THE LORD -
I HOPE AND PRAY -
THAT AN ANGEL WILL SEE THIS FOND ADIEU -
AND TELL YOU HOW MY HEART GRIEVED FOR THE LOSS OF YOU!
YET -
REJOICING!
KNOWING THAT NOW YOU ARE MORE FORTUNATE THAN I -
FOR NOW YOU NO LONGER HAVE TO SUFFER WITH A BROKEN WEARY HEART FROM THE STRAIN AND STRESS THIS WORLD INFLICTS ON US -
BUT NOW YOU ARE IN A NEW AND GLORIOUS BODY!
BUT NOW YOU ARE EVER IN THE JOY AND PRESENCE OF OUR LORD!
SO, MY BELOVED FRIEND -
I SHALL NOT MOURN -
I SHALL REJOICE!

AND PRAY THAT SOME DAY WE WILL MEET AGAIN,
AND NEVER BE SEPARATED -
BUT ETERNALLY WOVEN IN THE FABRIC OF EVER-
LASTING LIFE WITH OUR LORD!

(*Footnote)
In loving memory of my brother in the Lord - Mr. Bernie
Rubenstein - from Lovepower Music & Miracles Ministry in
Minneapolis, Mn. Who passed away 4/20/92 at 5:05 P.M.
Though his heart was weak, he showed this new Christian the fire
and boldness of faith in our Lord - Jesus Christ of Nazareth!

(Acknowledgment - I copied with my inserts to Mrs. Cowan's book - "Streams in the Desert" as my Holy Spirit revealed more deeply what the author expressed.)

THE TOMB OF LIFE!

WE ALL GO TO A LOVED ONE'S TOMB TO WEEP OVER THE GRAVE OF HIM OR HER WHO WAS THE BOSOM COMPANION OF OUR LIVES -
LET US GO BACK INTO A TIME IN HISTORY WHERE A YOUNG CARPENTER'S SON WALKED IN THE SHADOW OF OUR MORTAL SHELL -
THERE WAS A YOUNG WOMAN - MARY - EVERYONE THOUGHT MARY WAS GOING TO WEEP AT THE TOMB AND SO SHE DID;
BUT SHE HEARD THE MASTER HAD COME AND SHE WENT *FIRST TO HIM AND HE WENT WITH HER TO THE GRAVE.*!
HE WENT WITH HER FIRST TO WEEP AND THEN TO TURN HER MOURNING INTO JOY WITH LIFE FROM THE DEAD!

MY BELOVED -
WHATEVER WE MEAN TO DO, LET US *ALWAYS GO TO JESUS FIRST!*
ABBA FATHER GIVES US JESUS CHRIST OF NAZARETH AS OUR ELDER BROTHER -
IN HIM - WE HAVE THE BLESSED PRIVILEGE TO HAVE JESUS SYMPATHIZE WITH US IN OUR TIME OF GRIEV-ING AND MOURNING -
IN JESUS, HE IS OUR MEDIATOR -
THROUGH HIS BELOVED SON -
ABBA FATHER TELLS US IN THE SCRIPTURES -

"THY MAKER IS THINK HUSBAND!"
SO BELOVED MOURNER -
DO NOT WEEP -
HE KNOWS THE GRIEF AND ANGUISH YOU FEEL -
HE KNOWS THE DESOLATIONS OF YOUR SPIRIT AND
IT'S YEARNINGS AFTER A SOLACE THE WORLD CAN-
NOT GIVE TO YOU!
WHEN YOU GO TO THE GRAVE OF YOUR BELOVED ONE -
DO NOT LET YOUR TEARS, SO BLIND YOU, THAT YOU
CANNOT SEE THE TOMB IS EMPTY"!
NEITHER BELOVED -
HANG YOUR HEAD SO LOW THAT YOU CANNOT SEE
JESUS THERE AT THE TOMB WEEPING WITH YOU!

CAN YOU NOT SEE, BELOVED -
THAT HE HAS COME BESIDE YOU TO SUSTAIN YOU!
DO YOU NOT HEAR, BELOVED -
THE VERY WORDS OF LIFE AND HOPE -
"I AM THE RESURRECTION AND THE LIFE!"
CAN YOU SEE THRU THE TEARS THAT YOUR BELOVED
IS NOT DEAD -
THAT HIS OR HER BELIEVING SOUL THAT LIVED WITH
CHRIST HERE,
IS NOW LIVING WITH CHRIST IN HEAVEN AND THAT
HIS OR HER CHRISTIAN DUST IS SWEETLY SLEEPING.
ALL YOUR LOVE, AND WATCHING, AND ANXIOUSLY
NURSING COULD NOT SAVE HIM OR HER FROM SUF-
FERING AND SICKNESS AND THE TOMB -
BUT THE LOVE OF JESUS HAS DELIVERED HIM OR HER
FROM ALL SUFFERING,
SICKNESS AND DEATH!
HAVE YOU NOT HEARD JESUS SAY:
"I HAVE TAKEN DEATH'S STING AWAY!"
"FEAR NOT!"
JESUS CHRIST OF NAZARETH, OUR LORD, OUR SAVIOR,
OUR DELIVERER LAID DOWN HIS LIFE, HE LAID IN THE

SAME MORTAL TOMB AND HE SWEETENED IT FOR THE
SLEEP OF HIS BELOVED AND YOURS!

SO MY BELOVED -
WHEN YOU STOOP TO SEE WITHIN THE TOMB -
SEE THAT IT IS NOT A TOMB OF DEATH -
BUT OF LIFE!
OUR MASTER WHEN HE AROSE FROM THE MORTAL
TOMB OF DEATH OPENED A WAY THROUGH IT, UP
THROUGH IT, UP THROUGH THE RENT VEIL OF HEAVEN -
UP THROUGH THE EVERLASTING DOORS -
RIGHT INTO THE VERY GATES OF PARADISE!
DO YOU HEAR THE MASTER'S WORDS, BELOVED -
'I AM THE WAY, THE TRUTH, AND LIFE EVERLASTING!"
"ONLY BY ME, SHALL YOU SEE THE FATHER!"
THEREFORE, BELOVED -
SEEK THERE TO FOLLOW -
AND YOU WILL FIND THERE WAITING AT THE CELES-
TIAL GATES TO WELCOME YOU -
ONE MORE RADIANT THAN BEFORE IN WHOSE TRANS-
FIGURED COUNTENANCE,
YOU WILL RECOGNIZE HIM WHO THOU BELIEVEST
WAS LOST - BUT WHO HAS GONE BEFORE YOU TO OUR
FATHER'S HOUSE!

SO, ARISE, MY BELOVED!
PUT OFF THE GARMENTS OF HEAVINESS -
PUT OFF THE GARMENTS OF GLADNESS -
FOR I AM THE ENEMY'S TOMB OF DEATH -
FOR I AM YOUR TOMB OF EVERLASTING LIFE,

SO! COME! LET US REJOICE!
MY WORDS ARE LIFE UNTO THEE -
TAKE HOLD!
FOR MY PLANS FOR THEE ARE NOT EVIL BUT FOR
GOOD!

TRUST IN ME, BELOVED!
LOOK NOT AS THE WORLD WOULD SEE -
A TOMB FULL OF FEAR, BITTERNESS - DEATH!

(*Footnote)
Praise the Lord! Today, 7/28/94, started at 8:30 A.M., while reading "Deserts in the Stream," by Mrs. Cowan, there was a
particular passage, which the Holy Spirit took hold of me, He
illuminated even further the insight she received from Him.
For He spoke to me that there is someone in His house who is so
grieving, so mourning, death is at the doorstep, hungrily waiting
to steal that soul from the Lord's grasp. For this person, the Lord
is reaching out with arms to comfort, for in His very own words,
He speaks to His church.
In E ph. 5:29: "The Lord faithfully nourisheth and cherisheth His
church, His Bride."
That He calls Himself "her" husband, "her" precious, holy, affec-
tionate "husband".
(Is. 54:5) - "THY MAKER IS THINE HUSBAND!"
Here in the tomb of life He tells the reader that He knows the
grief and anguish we feel,
He knows the DESOLATIONS of our spirit and how it longs
after a comforting that this world
cannot give -
Only our God can comfort us in such moments in our lives!

There are those who have been abused physically and mentally
and emotionally by the very ones they loved and trusted.
There are those who have been raped as Tamar, Absalom's sister
in the accounting in Samuel, and then tossed out and hated.
The enemy has ripped at the very heart of these grieving, mourning souls -

Abba Father, Jesus Christ of Nazareth, and the Holy Spirit see this as the whitened fields of harvest that He describes in His Word -
The call of God is there -
"Pray to the Lord of the Harvest to send out the laborers"

So, my beloved friend, hear the call, walk in the shadow of our great and mighty God! For great are His everlasting mercies! Praise the Lord! Finished this at 10:35 A.M.

PROPHECY 10/18/94

BE STILL MY HEART - HEAR THE MASTER'S VOICE - HE BECKONS ME TO HIS SIDE - BY MY NAME, HE CALLS ME HIS BELOVED!

BE STILL MY HEART - THOUGH THE TEMPEST RAGES ROUND ABOUT THEE HEAR THE MASTER'S VOICE -
"BE STILL!"
"PEACE!"

HOW THE WAVES OF DESPAIR HARKEN TO THE MASTER'S COMMAND! HOW THE WINDS OF RAGE ARE LULLED TO CALMNESS BY THE MASTER'S VOICE!

OH! BE STILL MY POOR BROKEN HEART! FOR THE MASTER'S TOUCH IS UPON THEE! WITH THE BONDING OF HIS LOVE AND COMPASSION - WITH HIS TEARS AND TRAVAILING BLOODY SWEAT - HE FORGIVES MY TORN TWISTED SOUL! QUIETLY HE SPEAKS IN THE DEPTHS OF ME -
"BE STILL!"
"PEACE!"
"COME! BELOVED!"
"ALL IS WELL WITHIN THEE!"

(*Footnote)
Received this from my precious Adonai on 10/18/94 at 9:35 P.M.
Finished this at 9:40 P.M. Praise the Lord!

THE WHITE HARVEST!

EVENING TIDE

SEAGULLS CRYING IN THE SALTED BREEZE -
LIKE ACROBATS GRACEFULLY GLIDING UPON THE AIR
CURRENTS -
HIGH ABOVE THE BLUE-GREEN SEA -
THE SETTING BLAZING SUN SEEMINGLY DISAPPEAR-
ING INTO THE VASTNESS OF THE SEA -
SANDPIPERS LIKE SPIRITED BALLERINAS DANCING
UPON THE CREAMY SHORE -
A PEACEFUL LULL IN THE SOFT CARESSING WAVES -
EVENING-TIDE HAS COME TO SOFTLY KISS THE
SEAFOAMY SEA!
STARS TWINKLE IN THE PASTEL SKY -
ALL IS WELL, ALL IS WELL!
HOW MY SOUL SIGHS IN CONTENTMENT!

FIREFLY!

IN THE DEEPENING DUSK OF TWILIGHT -
GOLDEN JEWELS FLITTED ACROSS THE MEADOW!
ONE EVENING I CAUGHT ONE!
AND A TINY VOICE PLEADED:
"PLEASE LET ME GO!"
I LOOKED INTO MY CUPPED PALMS, AND TO MY
AMAZEMENT IT WAS ONLY A FIREFLY!
BUT AGAIN -
IN A TINY VOICE, IT SPOKE TO ME:
"HUMAN, DON'T CATCH MY BROTHERS AND SISTERS
EITHER!"
AND I SAID IN SURPRISE:
"WHY NOT?"
THE FIREFLY STOOD AS TALL AS IT COULD -
AND WITH A SURE BOLD VOICE IT STATED:
"THE LORD IS WALKING THIS EVENING IN HIS FIELDS -
"AND WE LIGHT HIS FOOTSTEPS SO HE WON'T STUM-
BLE AND FALL AND HURT HIMSELF!"
THEN I UNDERSTOOD!
THESE EVENING "JEWELS" CERTAINLY WERE THE
LORD'S SO I LET MY FIREFLY LOOSE -
AND QUICK AS A FLASH -
HE FLEW AWAY!
AND AS I LOOKED -
IT CERTAINLY SEEMED LIKE THEY WERE FOLLOWING
SOMEONE FOR HOW THEY GLOWED!
THESE "JEWELS" OF THE NIGHT!

(*Footnote)
Praise the Lord! Started this at 3:40 A.M. and finished at 3:45 A.M.

213

The Lord shows me that we are the fireflies, and that we are to be God's lamps, following the Lord wherever He leads us and to "capture" the desire of those who are in the evil night, to want our "light", and when they have "captured" us, they cannot do as they please with us, nor are we to let them do as they please with us or with one another.

For we are all children of the most high God! So why not become one of the Lord's firefly.

Just listen to His Voice calling you, drawing you near to Him. By His light in our lives and the Lord will put His golden "Sonlight" deep within you! Praise God!

THE BRIDAL COMPANY'S HOPE

LORD - I EXALT THEE!

JESUS, SWEET JESUS!
HOW GREAT THOU ART!
HOW WONDROUS IS YOUR LOVE FOR ME!
OH! ROSE OF SHARON -
HOW I DELIGHT IN THEE!
HOW TRULY WISDOM IS THE WINDOW THROUGH
WHICH YOUR GLORY SHINES FORTH!

PROPHECY 8/23/92

OH! COME! MY BELOVED CHILDREN -
IT IS TIME FOR JOY TO BE IN THE LAND!
IT IS NO LONGER TIME FOR SORROW -
FOR ALL YOUR ENEMIES THAT HAVE TORMENTED YOU
HAVE BEEN DEFEATED!
SO, COME, MY BELOVED CHILDREN -
DANCE WITH ME WITH JOY!
SING WITH ME THE SONGS OF VICTORY!
PRAISE WITH ME WITH LOVE UNENDING -
FOR REVIVAL IS IN THE LAND!
IT BEGINS, MY BELOVED, IN YOUR HEART,
FOR WHEN THERE IS PEACE WITH ME,
THERE IS PEACE ALL AROUND YOU,
THERE WILL BE PEACE IN YOUR HOUSEHOLD,
THERE WILL BE PEACE WITH YOUR NEIGHBORS,
THERE WILL BE PEACE IN YOUR COUNTRY,
THERE WILL BE PEACE IN THIS WORLD!
THIS, MY BELOVED, IS THE TRUE PEACE OF GOD!
NOT THE FALSE PEACE THAT IS IN THIS WORLD!
SO, BELOVED -
RAISE THE STANDARD OF VICTORY IN MY NAME,
AND YOU SHALL SEE WHAT A MIGHTY GOD IS IN THE
MIDST OF THEE!

COME! BELOVED!
ARISE!
FOR DAWN IS APPROACHING!
DO YOU NOT SEE THE BRIGHT MORNING STAR?
YES!
BELOVED, IT IS I, YOUR LORD AND KING!

BELOVED -
I AM HERE -
I SEE YOUR HEARTS -
I HEAR YOUR PLEAS -
BE STILL THIS MOMENT, MY BELOVED -
FOR YOU SHALL SEE MY GLORY!
YES, BELOVED -
I AM NOT ASLEEP -
FEAR NOT!
TREMBLE NOT!
I AM THE CAPTAIN OF THE HEAVENLY HOST!
THIS MOMENT, ALL WOLVES SHALL BECOME LEAN!
THE YOUNG LIONS WILL BE STILLED!
FOR A GLORIOUS MOMENT -
THERE WILL BE A SUMMER SEASON -
YOU ARE THE TREES OF EVERLASTING LIFE!
YOU ARE MY BROKEN MANNA -
YOU ARE MY WINE GIVEN AND POURED OUT TO THE
GUESTS I'VE CALLED TO FEAST AT MY TABLE!

SEE., BELOVED -
THE GIANTS TREMBLE -
FOR THEY SEE MY MIGHTY GIDEON!
FOR THEY SEE MY MIGHTY DAVID!
YES, BELOVED -
YOU ARE MY MIGHTY GLORIOUS BRIDE!
ARISE!
SHOUT VICTORY IN THE LAND!
THE ENEMY IS FLEEING BEFORE YOU AS YOU TAKE
BACK THIS LAND IN MY NAME!
SO, ARISE!
SING SONGS OF VICTORY!

PRAISE THE LORD!

SALT AND PEPPER!

AN ELDERLY GENTLEMAN WITH DISTINGUISHED
HEAD OF HAIR.
A CONDIMENT WE ADD TO OUR FOOD TO PLEASE OUR
PALATES.
BUT -
REALLY, MY FRIEND -
THERE IS MORE TO THIS!

IN AN ANCIENT BOOK WRITTEN A LONG TIME AGO -
THERE IS A MOST DISTURBING WARNING -
THERE IS A GENUINE COMPLIMENT TO STRETCH OUR
SOULS TO MATCH THIS WISE MAN'S EXPECTATIONS -
"YE ARE THE SALT OF THIS WORLD -
"IF THE SALT LOSES ITS FLAVOR, IT IS ONLY GOOD TO
BE TRAMPLED UNDERFOOT...-"
WHAT WISDOM DOES THE AUTHOR POSSESS!
FOR I IN MY SMALL WORLD OF CARNAL SENSES, CAN-
NOT EVEN BEGIN TO FATHOM THE MEANING - LET
ALONE - THE UNDERSTANDING OF SUCH THOUGHTS!

THEN LO!
THE HOLY SPIRIT OF THE LIVING AUTHOR WHISPERS
INTO THE VERY DEPTHS OF MY BEING -
"MAN, CAN YOUR THOUGHTS BE MY THOUGHTS?"
"MAN, CAN MY THOUGHTS BE YOUR THOUGHTS?"
"COME! LET US REASON TOGETHER AND SEEK YE THE
FRUIT OF WISDOM,
"THERE TO BE FOUND IN MY GARDEN, GROWING ON
THE TREE OF LIFE -
"FOR THE BEGINNING OF KNOWING WHO I AM, WILL

BE THE BEGINNING OF "FEAR THIS THEN WILL BE
TRULY THE BEGINNING OF KNOWLEDGE!"
FOR "I AM" HE WHO BREATHES INTO YOUR SOUL MY
LIFE -
"AND I HAVE FASHIONED YOU INTO MY IMAGE -
"I HAVE SOUGHT THEE FROM THE ENDS OF THE
EARTH!
"YEA"
"EVEN UNTO THE DEPTHS OF THE SEA!
"FOR YOU ARE MY SALT OF THIS EARTH!"

THEN THERE WAS VERY DEEP STILLNESS IN THE VERY
ECHOING EMPTINESS OF MY SOUL -
WHO SPOKE TO ME?
AT FIRST - IT WAS LIKE A WHISPER OF A BREEZE -
THEN IT'S VOICE GROWING TO A THUNDEROUS ROAR
OF A WATERFALL RAPIDS -
"IT" RESPONDED TO MY HEART'S QUESTION:

"I AM!"
I FELL TO MY FACE -
STUNNED SO STILL AS TO APPEAR DEAD FOR WIS-
DOM'S VOICE SPOKE AND GAVE ME FULL
UNDERSTANDING TO ALL MY PONDERING SOUL
ANGUISHED CRIES -
THE VOICE WITHIN ME IS THE VERY AUTHOR OF THAT
ANCIENT BOOK -
                    THE LORD OF HEAVENS!
"LORD!" I CRIED OUT -
"WHAT ARE YOU SAYING IN YOUR BOOK OF TRUTH
AND LIFE ABOUT US -
"THE CHILDREN OF THIS EARTH - THIS WORLD BEING
THE "SALT OF THIS WORLD?"
AGAIN, EVER SO GENTLE -
AS THOUGH A FATHER WAS TEACHING HIS PRECIOUS
LITTLE ONE -

HE REPLIED:

"IN THIS MODERN, HIGH TECH WORLD YOU LIVE IN -

"IN THIS HIGHEST PINNACLE OF MAN'S ACCOMPLISH-
MENT -

"ON THE VERY BRINK OF ABSOLUTES -

"YOUR HEARTS HAVE BECOME STONE COLD TOWARDS
ONE ANOTHER!

"WHERE, OH! MAN, IS THY HEART OF FLESH THAT I
HAVE CREATED WITHIN YOU?

"WHERE, OH! MAN, ARE THE WORDS I HAVE INSCRIBED
ON THAT HEART -

"MY LAWS AND PRECEPTS -

"GIVEN TO YOU AT A GREAT COST?"

"FROM THE FIRST BREATH YOU BREATHED -

"I INSTILLED WITHIN YOU THE VERY NATURE OF MY
BEING -

"YET -

"YOU HAVE DARED TO RISE ABOVE THY CREATOR?

"FOR WITH ARROGANT VOICES, YOU SHOUT TO THE
HEAVENS - 'WE ARE "gods!"

"THY PUNGENT FRAGRANCE OF PRIDE AND ABOMINA-
TIONS I WILL NOT CONSUME!

"WHERE, OH! MAN, IS THE SALT OF YOUR TEARS FOR
YOUR FELLOW BROTHERS?

"IS THERE NO COMPASSION TO FLAVOR THE BITTER-
NESS LEFT FROM THE ENEMY'S MEAL OF PRIDE?

"NOW, YOU HAVE BECOME THE VERY LIKENESS OF MY
ADVERSARY -

"LOST ARE MY PRECIOUS CHILDREN -

"FOR THE SALT HAS BECOME THE PEPPER OF THIS
WORLD!"

"WHO OF YOU, OH! MAN, HAS THE TRUE SALT TO FLA-
VOR THY ENEMY'S BITTER BREAD OF LIFE?

"MUST YOU ALSO POISON IT WITH THE PEPPERINESS
OF YOUR CRUELTY?

"IF THERE BE NO MORE SALT IN THIS WORLD -

"THEN I WILL COME, AND I WILL TRAMPLE YOU TO THE DUST I HAVE CREATED YOU FROM -

"AND I WILL SHAKE OFF FROM MY FEET OF THY PUNGENT ODOR OF REBELLION -

"FOR HOW CAN THE STUDENT BE GREATER THAN THE MASTER?

"GODS" YOU CRY OUT!

"YET THE VERY EARTH IS CRYING OUT FOR THY FOUL DEEDS DONE IN THE SECRET OF THY STONY HEARTS -

"I AM HE WHO WILL COME TO BRING LIGHT INTO YOUR DARKNESS -

"FOR WHAT FELLOWSHIP CAN LIGHT HAVE WITH DARKNESS?

"THOSE OF YOU WHO FLAVOR THIS WORLD WITH YOUR TEARS, I WILL COME WITH MY REWARDS,

"I WILL GATHER YOU FROM THE FOUR CORNERS OF THIS WORLD, EVEN UNTO THE VERY DEPTHS OF THE SEA -

"AND I WILL GIVE YOU REST,

AND I WILL REFRESH YOUR SOULS,

AND I WILL GIVE THEE A CROWN OF EVERLASTING LIFE TO DWELL IN MY TEMPLE FOREVER!"

"BUT THOSE OF YOU WHO SPRINKLE THIS EARTH WITH YOUR PUNGENT ARROGANCE AND REBELLION -

"BEWARE - FOR I AM COMING WITH A MIGHTY SICKLE!

"JUDGMENT IS UPON THEE, OH! MAN!"

(*Footnotes)
Praise the Lord, for His goodness and mercy lasts forever! Started this on 8/16/96 at 4:00 A M. Finished this at 4:35 A.M.

"lord - help me to always be the salt of this world, and not the bitter pepper to be used by your enemy to poison my fellow brothers and sisters, in your most holy, precious name, Oh! Jesus of

222

Nazareth, I pray!

Amen!

Praise the Lord of the heavens with all of your hearts, Oh! Saints of God!

CRIMSON GLOW

HOW STRANGE IS OUR LUNAR NIGHT-LITE!
FOR IT HAS NO LIGHT OF ITS OWN -
IT JUST REFLECTS THE PALE SUNLIGHT!
YET -
SOME RARE EVENINGS -
THERE IS A CRIMSON GLOW!
WHOSE BLOODY REFLECTION DOES SHE REFLECT?
COULD SHE POSSIBLY BE REFLECTING THE BLOODY
VIOLENT EARTH'S LIGHT?
SINCE THE CREATION OF MAN -
THE EARTH TASTED HER FIRST VIOLENT WINE OF
DEATH!
HOW LOW HAS THE INHABITANTS OF THIS PLANET
EVOLVED INTO?
HERE WE ARE AT THE VERY BRINK OF A NEW MILLEN-
NIUM -
THERE ARE SOCIAL CULTURES MAKING BRASH STATE-
MENTS THAT MANKIND IS HAVING IT'S FINAL STEP OF
EVOLUTION - WE ARE BECOMING "gods"!

YET -
WHY ARE THE CEMETERIES OVERBOUNDING WITH
HEART-RENDING EPITAPHS OF A LOVED ONE?
YET -
EVEN OUR FORESTS -
EVEN OUR RIVERS -
EVEN OUR LAKES -
EVEN OUR SEA -
THERE ARE SECRET BURIAL GROUNDS, WATERY
GRAVES OF VIOLENT BLOODSHED!

I CAME ACROSS AN ANCIENT BOOK -
IN ITS FINAL CHAPTER -
A WARNING IS ISSUED:
"IN THE END TIMES, THE EARTH WILL GRIEVE FOR IT'S DEAD -
"THEY THAT HAVE NOT RECEIVED THE SON OF MAN AS THEIR SAVIOR, THEIR LORD AND KING -
"SHALL BE CAST OUT FROM THE MESSIAH'S KINGDOM OF ETERNAL LIFE -
"THESE SIGNS SHALL COME TO PASS, JUST AS A WOMAN WHO KNOWS IT IS TIME TO GIVE BIRTH WILL CRY OUT IN THE BEGINNING PANGS OF LABOR -
"SO SHALL THE HOLY ONE OF ISRAEL, SHALL CRY OUT WITH A LOUD SHOUT:
"NO LONGER WILL I BE GRIEVED BY YOUR REBEL-LIOUS, MURDEROUS HEARTS -
"YOU SHALL RECEIVE THE VENGEANCE OF THY TRUE FATHER -
"FOR FROM THE BEGINNING OF THE FOUNDATION OF TIME -
"HE WAS A MURDERER, A LIAR, AND A THIEF -
"WHEN YOU SEE THE SIGNS AND WONDERS IN THE HEAVENS -
"THE SUN WILL BECOME DARKENED -
"THE MOON WILL BECOME BLOOD RED -
"THE STARS WILL FALL FROM THE HEAVENS -
"THERE IN THE CLOUDS WITH A MULTITUDE OF THOSE WHOSE GARMENTS HAVE BEEN WASHED IN THE BLOOD OF THE HOLY LAMB OF GOD -
"SHALL BE SEEN BY ALL THE NATIONS, TRIBES, AND PEOPLES OF THIS EARTH -
"THERE IN THE MIDST -
"THE SON OF MAN - RETURNS!"
"WITH A DOUBLE-EDGED SWORD IN HIS MOUTH -
"THE DEAD SHALL RISE FIRST TO MEET AND GREET THEIR LONG AWAITED MESSIAH!

"THEN THEY THAT HAVE BEEN CALLED AND CHOSEN, SHALL ALSO GREET THEIR KING AS A BLUSHING BRIDE" -
"CLOTHED IN RAIMENT OF PURE WHITE LINEN, A CLOAK OF CRIMSON,
CROWNED WITH GLORY OF HER BELOVED BRIDE-GROOM -
WE, HIS PEOPLE, HIS BELOVED BRIDE -
SHALL RISE UP TO GREET OUR LORD, TO RETURN TO OUR RIGHTFUL HOME -
NEVER TO TASTE SORROW AGAIN -
NEVER TO FEEL DEATH'S BITTER STING -
NEVER TO SHED A TEAR OF GRIEF -
REJOICING, SINGING SONGS OF PRAISE AND ADORA-TION -
WE WILL REFLECT THE SON'S GLORY FOREVER -
YET -
THOSE WHO ARE MURDERERS, LIARS, THIEVES, IDOL-ATORS, SHALL NEVER ENTER THIS KINGDOM!

SO, MY FRIEND -
WHEN YOU ARE LOOKING UP AT THE NIGHT SKY -
AND YOU SHOULD SEE A CRIMSON MOON -
FALL UPON YOUR FACE, AND CRY OUT FORGIVENESS AND MERCY TO HIM WHOM WE SHOULD FEAR -
FOR HE IS THE ONE WHO CAN KILL BOTH THE BODY AND THE SOUL!
BUT IF THE SON OF MAN, JESUS CHRIST OF NAZARETH IS YOUR LORD AND SAVIOR -
THEN ON A BATED BREATH -
HOPE FOR HIS RETURN TO BE QUICKLY -
FOR THE SON IS BECOMING DARKENED BY THE REFLECTION OF OUR BLOODY DEEDS -
BY OUR STONE COLD HEARTS TOWARDS ONE ANOTH-ER,
BY OUR WORSHIPPING "gods" WE HAVE CREATED WITH

OUR HANDS AND IMAGINATIONS -
BEWARE!
OUR GOD IS ONE, OUR GOD IS HOLY, OUR GOD IS A
JEALOUS GOD,
HE WILL NOT HAVE ANY OTHER "gods" BEFORE HIM!
WE ARE STOKING THE FATHER'S ANGER BY OUR
SECRET DEEDS -
IN ARROGANCE WE SAY: "WHO WILL SEE OUR DEEDS?
WHO WILL CONDEMN US?"
READER - THE HOLY ONE OF ISRAEL - THE TRUE LIV-
ING GOD - WILL!

(*Footnote)
Praise God! Bless the Lord Oh! my soul! Started this on 9/27/96
at 2:00 A.M. Finished this at 2:30 A.M. here at work! Praise the
Lord! Hallelujah!

THE MARRIAGE FEAST!

HEAVENLY VISION

"COME, BELOVED!
"COME MY SISTER, MY BRIDE!"
"COME!"

I LOOKED AROUND ME, I COULD HEAR HIS SOFT COM-
MANDING VOICE -
TUGGING IN MY HEART -
THERE HE WAS -
RIGHT BESIDE ME!
BATHED IN WARM GOLDEN LIGHT -
THE SUN WAS DIM COMPARED TO THAT LIGHT!
HIS AZURE EYES SPARKLED -
HIS SMILE SHONE LIKE POLISHED MARBLE -
HE REACHED OUT HIS HAND TO ME -
"COME!"
"MY BELOVED!"
"COME!"
"I HAVE BEEN WAITING FOR YOU!"

I PLACED MY SMALL HAND INTO HIS LARGE YET GEN-
TLE HAND -
WE BEGAN TO GLIDE UPWARD TOWARDS THE CELES-
TIAL CEILING OF THIS WORLD!
THERE AMONG THE CLOUDS, A SILVERY STAIRWAY
APPEARED!
ANGELS IN RADIANT WHITE GARMENTS FLANKED
EACH SIDE -
EACH ANGEL HAD IN HIS HAND A MUSICAL INSTRU-
MENT -
ANGELS WITH TRUMPETS OF GOLD -

ANGELS WITH HARPS OF SILKEN CORDS -
ANGELS WITH TAMBOURINES WITH SILVER CLAPPERS -
ALL SINGING IN ONE HARMONIOUS CHORUS!
"SING ALL YOU PEOPLE OF THE EARTH!"
"SING ALL YOU PEOPLE -
"THE KING HAS COME FOR HIS BRIDE!"
"REJOICE, ALL YE NATIONS -
"THE KING HAS COME TO RULE AND REIGN IN ALL HIS
RIGHTEOUS GLORY!"
"REJOICE, ALL YE BRIDES OF THE LORD!"
"COME!"
"THE WEDDING FEAST HAS BEEN PREPARED!"
"COME!"
"ALLELUJAH!"
"ALLELUJAH!"
"SING ALL YE NATIONS!"
"THE KING HAS COME TO CLAIM HIS BRIDE!"

(*Footnotes)
Received this on 7/21/90 at 11:40 P.M. I was at Donna's house at
that moment of the vision!

THE BRIDEGROOM'S CALL TO HIS BRIDE!

MY BELOVED -
DO NOT FEAR -
THOUGH IT BE NIGHT -
FILLED WITH THE TERRORS OF YOUR FEARS -
FEAR NOT!
FOR I AM WITH YOU -
NOT JUST FOR A MOMENT -
NOT WHEN YOU CRY OUT IN SHEER DESPERATE HOPE-
LESSNESS -
I AM WITH YOU!

WHEN YOU ARISE AND BEGIN THE DAY -
COME TO ME -
I WILL GIVE YOU STRENGTH TO FACE THE THORNS
AND THE WOLVES THAT WOULD TEAR AT YOU!
WHEN A SEEKING HEART QUESTIONS YOUR PEACE-
FULNESS IN A TIME OF TURMOIL AND CONFUSION -
TOGETHER, WE CAN SHOW THE WAY TO HOPE AND
PEACE!
DID I NOT SAY TO YOU THAT I WILL GIVE YOU PEACE -
NOT AS THE WORLD UNDERSTANDS AND DESIRES -
BUT MY PEACE WHICH IS FAR MORE SURPASSING
EVEN TO YOUR UNDERSTANDING!

AND WHEN EVENING TIME COMES -
LET US TOGETHER SUP BY THE SHORES OF GALILEE!
LET MY HEALING BALM SOOTHE AND BATHE YOU -

WHEN NIGHT APPROACHES -
DO NOT FEAR OF THE SHADOWS THAT WALK IN THE
VALLEY OF DEATH -
FOR I AM WITH YOU!

SO MY BELOVED -
FEAR NOT!
TRUST ME IMPLICITLY!
LET ME GUIDE YOU THROUGH THE TEMPESTS OF LIFE!
LET ME BE YOUR ROCK -
ANCHOR THYSELF DEEPLY WITHIN THE FOUNDATION
OF MY WORD -
AND NO WINDS OF FURIOUS HATE -
NO WINDS OF CUTTING JEALOUSY -
NO WINDS OF CRUSHING CHANGES -
WILL CAUSE YOU TO BE LOOSENED FROM ME!
AS YOU WILLINGLY AND LOVINGLY SURRENDER
YOUR WILL, AND SERVE ME -
YOU WILL BE IN MY FATHER'S INNER SANCTUARY, HIS
WINGS WILL COVER YOU -
NO ENEMIES -
NO WEAPONS FORMED AGAINST YOU -
NO GATES OF HELL SHALL PREVAIL AGAINST YOU!

COME!
MY BELOVED!
COME REST BY MY SIDE -
WHEN THE BURDENS OF THIS WORLD WEIGHS SO
HEAVILY UPON YOU -
AND YOU SHOULD FALL TO YOUR KNEES -
AND OUR ENEMIES ARE SCORNING AND MOCKING
YOU -
LOOK TO THE CROSS OF CALVARY!
THERE YOU WILL SEE YOUR VICTORY AND YOUR
SALVATION!
THERE UPON THAT ACCURSED TREE OF DEATH -

THE ENEMY'S POWER OVER YOU IS SHATTERED!
HIS STING OF DEATH -
I'VE TAKEN UPON MYSELF -
WILLINGLY -
LOVINGLY -
FOR I AM YOUR LIFE!
ETERNAL LIFE!
FOR MY BELOVED -
NO GREATER LOVE IS THERE, EXCEPT THAT WHICH
ONE LAYS DOWN HIS LIFE FOR ANOTHER!

COME, MY BELOVED LITTLE ONE -
THOUGH IT BE A TIME OF MOURNING AND SORROW -
THOUGH IT BE A TIME TO TRAVAIL FOR ONE ANOTHER -
REMEMBER -
THE. WORLD HATED ME BECAUSE THEY DID NOT
KNOW ME -
FOR I HAVE NOT COME FROM THE WORLD -
BUT, MY FATHER HAS SENT ME TO BE THE BRIGHT
MORNING STAR IN A WORLD FILLED WITH BITTER
COLD NIGHT!

I AM THE LION OF THE TRIBE OF JUDAH -
HEAR MY MIGHTY ROAR OF VICTORY IN THE LAND!
SEE OUR ENEMIES FLEE!
I AM YOUR DELIVERER IN TIMES OF TRIBULATION!
I AM YOUR PROTECTOR IN TIMES OF PERSECUTION!
I AM YOUR PHYSICIAN IN TIMES WHEN THE ENEMY
TEARS AT YOU!
I AM YOUR COUNSELOR IN TIMES OF HOPELESSNESS!
I AM!
SO I TOLD MOSES AT THE BURNING BUSH,
SO TOO, MY BELOVED, I AM SPEAKING TO YOU!
SO! BE OF GOOD CHEER!
REJOICE!
FOR YOUR KING IS RETURNING FOR HIS BELOVED

TRUE WARRIOR BRIDE!
YES, BELOVED -
IT IS BY MY SPIRIT -
NOT BY YOUR MIGHT -
NOR BY YOUR POWER -
BUT BY YOUR PRAISES -
BY YOUR TRAVAILING IN BENT KNEE HEART INTER-
CESSION FOR EACH OTHER -
IS THE BATTLE FOUGHT AND WON -
TO BRING HOME -
THE LOST -
THE BLIND AND DEAF -
THE WOUNDED CHILDREN OF MY FATHER'S KINGDOM!

SO, MY BELOVED -
I SPEAK INTO THE VERY INNER CHAMBERS OF YOUR
HEART -
BE NOT FEARFUL -
BE NOT WEARY OR FAINT-HEARTED -
I AM COMING QUICKLY -
AND WITH ME, I BRING YOUR REWARD -
A CROWN OF EVERLASTING LIFE!
I WILL COME AND WIPE AWAY YOUR TEARS!
I WILL COME AND FILL YOUR EMPTINESS WITH JOY!
NO LONGER WILL YOU MOURN AND GRIEVE!
SO, MY BELOVED,
TAKE MY HAND,
LET US LABOR FOR AWHILE LONGER -
WHEN THE MIDNIGHT HOUR IS UPON THEE -
WATCH!
BE ALERT!
SOUND THE TRUMPET!
SEE!
NIGHT HAS BEEN OVERCOME BY THE DAWNING OF
YOUR SALVATION!
I AM YOUR MESSIAH!

I AM YOUR BRIDEGROOM!
COME LET US GO TO THE MARRIAGE FEAST -
ALL THE GUESTS ARE COMING -
THOSE WHO REJECT THE INVITATION -
SHALL BE LOCKED OUT OF MY FATHER'S HOUSE -
FOR WHAT FELLOWSHIP HAS LIGHT WITH DARKNESS?
THOSE WHO HAVE REJECTED THE INVITATION TO
COME -
ARE THE CHILDREN OF THE DARK -
AND THEY WILL HAVE THE SAME FINAL JUDGMENT AS
THEIR FATHER - satan -
FOR he IS THE father OF LIES!

satan!
THE ACCUSER OF THE BRETHREN -
THEY SHALL ALL BE THROWN INTO THE LAKE OF FIRE!
THEY SHALL NEVER WOUND, TEAR, MURDER, STEAL
FROM THOSE WHOM I'VE INHERITED!
WHEN I GLORIFIED MY FATHER -
UPON THE HILL OF GOLGOTHA -
UPON THE CROSS OF VICTORY -
I HAVE PAID THE PRICE FOR YOUR REDEMPTION!
NONE SHALL I LOSE!
SO. MY BELOVED, BE STEADFAST!
SET YOUR JAW FIRMLY FORWARD -
NEITHER LOOK TO THE RIGHT OR TO THE LEFT -
BE NOT LURED TO GO ON THE BROAD PATH OF
DESTRUCTION -
FOR MANY TRAVEL THAT PATH, HEEDING TO THEIR
OWN WISDOM -
YET -
THEY WILL ONLY LEAD YOU TO EVERLASTING
DAMNATION AND DESTRUCTION OF YOUR SOUL!
SO, MY PRECIOUS LITTLE ONE -
STAY ON THE NARROW PATH -
THOUGH IT BE SHADOWED AND FULL OF UNSEEN ENE-

MIES -
BE NOT AFRAID!

FOR WE TRAVEL THIS PATH TOGETHER!
NO HARM WILL COME UPON THEE!
BELOVED, STAY ON THE NARROW PATH, THOUGH IT
APPEARS EXTREMELY DANGEROUS -
FEAR NOT!
MY HOLY SPIRIT WILL GUIDE YOU SAFELY THROUGH
TO MY KINGDOM!
LET MY WORDS BE YOUR LAMP TO GUIDE YOUR FOOT-
STEPS -
HOME IS BUT A FAITH STONE'S THROW ACROSS THE
CHAOS OF TIME!
THERE YOU WILL AT LAST SEE ME CLEARLY -
THERE YOU WILL UNDERSTAND ALL THINGS I'VE SPO-
KEN TO YOU THROUGH THE ROUGH SEAS OF LIFE!
FOR THIS IS BUT A MOMENT -
LIKE THE GRASS IT WILL WITHER AND DIE
BUT IN A TWINKLING OF AN EYE -
YOU SHALL BE IN YOUR NEW GLORIOUS BEING -
AS YOU WERE CREATED IN OUR IMAGE -
I HAVE CREATED YOU!
REJOICE!
DAWN IS QUICKLY APPROACHING -
YOUR KING AND HIS HEAVENLY HOSTS FILL THE
HEAVENS FOR ALL TO SEE HIS GLORY!

(*Footnotes)
Praise the Lord! Started this at midnight Dec. 12, 1993. Finished
this at 1 07 A.M.

PROPHECY 1 1/21/92

OH! PREPARE THYSELVES, MY BELOVED CHILDREN -
FOR GREAT IS THE DAY OF THE KING'S RETURN!
SOON OLD THINGS WILL PASS AWAY -
AND MY HOLY CITY SHALL DWELL AMONGST MEN!

SEE, MY BELOVED -
I SHALL CREATE A NEW HEAVEN AND A NEW EARTH -
OLD THINGS WILL BE WIPED AWAY -
THERE WILL BE NO MORE TEARS -
THERE WILL BE NO MORE SORROW -
THERE WILL BE NO MORE HUNGER OR THIRST -
FOR IN MY NEW JERUSALEM -
I WILL DWELL AMONGST THEE -
I WILL BE YOUR GOD -
AND YE SHALL BE MY HOLY PEOPLE
SO, COME!
PREPARE THYSELVES, FOR THE BRIDEGROOM QUICK-
LY APPROACHES TO GATHER HIS BELOVED BRIDE!
THE MARRIAGE FEAST IS LAID OUT -
THE GUESTS HAVE BEEN CALLED -
SO, COME MY BELOVED -
SIT BY MY SIDE -
LET US REIGN IN MY NEW KINGDOM TOGETHER -
FOR THIS IS YOUR RIGHTFUL INHERITANCE -
FOR THIS PURPOSE I HAVE CREATED THEE!

(*Footnote)
Praise the Lord! On 1 1/21/92 at 8:00 A.M. I awoke from a dream
where I was talking to Pastor David telling him that just before
the bomb detonated, I heard:

"I SHALL CREATE A NEW HEAVEN AND A NEW EARTH."
Then a loud voice yelled:
"Hit the ground!" I awoke coughing, choking, gagging and this prophecy came. Oh! My God! Have mercy on your people! Amen!

OF REWARDS
AND JUDGMENTS

INTO THE MOUTH OF DEATH!
BY JESUS OF NAZARETH, MY SAVIOR!

COME, MY BELOVED!
COME, FOLLOW ME!
I WILL TAKE YOU ON A JOURNEY OF IMMEASURABLE
SORROW!
FOR YOU SEE, MY BELOVED,
YOU MUST SEE WITH MY EYES -
YOU MUST FEEL MY ACHE EACH TIME I LOSE A LOST
WOUNDED LAMB!
YOU MUST SHED MY TEARS OF COMPASSION FOR ALL
WHO ARE IN DARKNESS -
YOU MUST WALK IN MY FOOTSTEPS -
SO YOU CAN GIVE MY NEW FRESH BREATH OF LIFE TO
MY SLEEPING SHEEP!
DO NOT FEAR, MY BELOVED!
I WILL BE WITH YOU ON THIS JOURNEY -
CLING ONTO ME AS THAT OF A DROWNING SOUL
CLINGS FOR LIFE ONTO THE ROPE OF RESCUE!
DO NOT TRY TO SWIM TOWARDS THE SAFE HARBOR,
RATHER TRUST ME THAT I WILL SAVE YOU!

"YES, MY LORD!"
"I WILL FOLLOW YOU"!
"I WILL CLING ONLY UNTO YOU THROUGHOUT THIS
JOURNEY!"
"I WILL NOT HAVE ANY FEAR, FOR I TRUST THAT YOU
ARE ALWAYS NEAR ME!"
I LOOKED UP INTO HIS SAD TEAR-FILLED EYES -
TEARS WERE WELLING INTO THOSE DEEP POOLS OF
SEA-MIST,

YET -

HE SMILED TENDERLY AND LOVINGLY AT ME!

HE GENTLY TOOK MY TINY HAND, AND WE STEPPED OUT ONTO THE BALCONY, THE AIR WAS CLEAN AND CRISP -

A GENTLE BREEZE FROM THE LAKE RUFFLED INTO OUR HAIR -

UPWARDS WE GLIDED, THE EARTH SWIFTLY RECEDED FAR BELOW THERE IN THE STARRY BLACK VOID -

WITH THE SUN ON THE RIGHT OF US -

THE MOON ON THE LEFT -

THE WONDROUS ORDERLY FIRMAMENT ROUND ABOUT US -

IN AWE, I LOOKED DOWN ON THIS BEAUTIFUL, COLORFUL, UNIQUE PLANET GOD GAVE US!

BUT THERE IT WOULD SEEM -

STRETCHED OUT ON THE SURFACE OF THE EARTH A BLACKNESS LOOMED UPON IT!

IN A PUZZLED WAY -

I LOOKED AT MY LORD -

BUT BEFORE I COULD SPEAK -

HE SADLY SPOKE WITHIN ME -

"YES, THERE IS THE ENEMY -

"SEE HOW HE GROWS!"

"WITH EACH PASSING MOMENT, HE DEVOURS MY FLOCK, AND HE GROWS EVER STRONGER!"

I LOOKED DOWN AT THE WORLD FAR BELOW US, FOR I DID NOT UNDERSTAND WHAT MY LORD WAS SPEAKING ABOUT,

THEN -

I SAW THE BLACKNESS HE REFERRED TO AS THAT OF A MAN-SHAPED FORM!

MY LORD AND I, GLIDED DOWN TOWARDS THAT HORRIBLE DARKNESS TOWARDS ITS HUGE MOUTH!

FEAR CHILLED THROUGH ME, AND I BEGAN TO DESPERATELY CLING TO MY SAVIOR!

"LORD, MUST WE GO INTO THAT GAPING MAW OF DEATH?"
"YES, MY BELOVED!"
"THIS IS THE JOURNEY OF SORROW I SPOKE ABOUT!"

INTO THE DARKEST DARK MOUTH OF FEAR WE GLIDED INTO -
THE STENCH WAS UNBREATHABLE, I FELT MY LUNGS DESPERATELY TRYING TO GASP CLEAN AIR!
ALL AROUND US THE AIR CLUNG UNTO US AS A SUFFOCATING CLOAK, HEAT ROSE UP FROM DEEP WITHIN THIS HUGE CAVERN -
AS MY FEET TOUCHED THE GROUND -
I WAS IMMEDIATELY REPULSED BY THE TOUCH!
A BONE-SEARING COLDNESS SEEPED THROUGH THEM -
IMMENSE FEAR WELLED UP INTO MY HEART -
AS A DROWNING PERSON CRIES OUT FOR HELP, SO TOO, I CRIED OUT:
"JESUS OF NAZARETH, MY LORD AND SAVIOR!"
"HELP ME!"
IMMEDIATELY HIS WARM LIFE ENVELOPED ME -
HIS STRENGTH FILLING THE PLACES WHERE DEATH TOUCHED ME!
EVER DOWNWARD WE WENT TILL FINALLY I BEGAN TO HEAR FAINT SOUNDS COMING FROM DEEP INTO THIS DARK PIT -
FINALLY, I BEGAN TO SEE A FAINT YELLOW-RED GLOW EMANATING FROM THE END OF THIS HUGE CAVE -
AS WE WENT EVER DEEPER, THE SOUND INCREASED IN VOLUME -
THE GLOW INCREASED TO PAINFUL HEAT-SEARING LIGHT!
OH! MY GOD!
ITS A HUMAN VOICE SCREAMING IN TORMENTED AGONY!

I HUNG ONTO MY JESUS SO TIGHTLY!
I LOOKED AT HIS FACE -
HIS SWEET VISAGE WAS NOW STERNLY SOMBER -
TEARS STREAMED DOWN HIS HIGH CHEEKS -
I HEARD HIS SOFT WHISPER DEEP WITHIN ME -
A WHISPER SO HEAVY WITH SORROW -
I FELT HIS ACHE DEEP WITHIN MY HEART -
IT FELT LIKE A PORCELAIN SHELL READY TO BURST
AND BLEED!
IN A VOICE FILLED WITH EMOTIONS, HE SPOKE TO ME -
"SEE, MY BELOVED -
"HERE IS ONE OF MY LOST SHEEP!
"SHE WAS SO VERY BLESSED,
"BUT SHE ALSO LOVED THE ADORATION OF THIS
WORLD MORE THAN SHE LOVED ME!
I LOOKED AT THIS MISERABLE TORTURED SOUL -
THERE WAS NO BEAUTY -
ONLY TATTERED REMNANTS OF FLESH HANGING
LOOSELY ON HER FRAIL SKELETAL FRAME, SHE CRIED
OUT IN A SHRIEK FULL OF ANGUISH AND SUPPLICA-
TION -
"MY LORD!"
"HELP ME!"
"SAVE ME "!
"TAKE ME AWAY FROM THIS PLACE OF ETERNAL TOR-
MENT!"
JESUS, QUIETLY SPOKE TO HER:
"DAUGHTER, WHEN YOU WERE AMONGST THE LIVING,
DID I NOT SUPPLY ALL YOUR NEEDS?"
"DID NOT MY LABORERS COME TO YOU AND TAUGHT
YOU THE PATH INTO MY KINGDOM?"
"DID YOU NOT ONCE SAY - 'I LOVE YOU, LORD, BUT
TODAY I CANNOT WALK WITH YOU! -
'I LOVE YOU, LORD, BUT TODAY I CANNOT TALK WITH
YOU FOR I HAVE SO MUCH TO DO!"!
"OH! YES, MY LORD, THOSE WERE MY FOOLISH

WORDS!"

"I WAS SO NEEDED BY MY WORK, MY FRIENDS, MY FAMILY -

"THERE JUST WASN'T ANY TIME TO LISTEN AND FOLLOW YOU!"

SUDDENLY!

THIS FIENDISH DARK DISTORTED FORM CAME BETWEEN US!

IT'S BEADY FIERY EYES LOCKED UPON MY LORD -

IN A RASPY IRRITATING VOICE, IT SPOKE ARROGANTLY -

"YOU HAVE NO AUTHORITY HERE!"

"I HAVE WON HER AWAY FROM YOU!"

"BY YOUR FINAL JUDGMENT UPON HER -

"SHE IS MINE"!

AT THIS, THE CREATURE TURNED AND DRAMATICALLY RAISED IT'S DEFORMED ARMS AND IMMEDIATELY THE IMMENSE FLESH-SEARING FLAMES AROSE UP FROM THE GROUND SHROUDING THE WITHERING WOMAN IN TORMENTED AGONY -

HER SHRIEKING WAILS WERE SO UNBEARABLE, I COVERED MY EARS AND I LAID MY HEAD UPON MY JESUS CHEST!

"OH! LORD!"

I SOBBED INTO HIS HUGE SOFT CHEST -

THE CREATURE LAUGHED HEINOUSLY.

INSTANTLY, WE WERE GONE FROM THAT HORRIBLE SCENE -

YET, HER TORMENTED WAILS ECHOED AND RE-ECHOED WITHIN AND AROUND ME!

(4/29/90)

COME, MY BELOVED!

FEAR NOT! I AM WITH YOU ALWAYS!

ONCE AGAIN, DOWNWARD WE GLIDED IN THAT FOOLISH DARK MOUTH OF DEATH -

TILL ONCE AGAIN, THERE WAS A FAINT GLOW -

246

TILL ONCE AGAIN, I COULD HEAR THE TORMENTED SCREECHES OF AGONY!

BUT THIS TIME THERE WERE SEVERAL VOICES, ALL RISING TO A CRESCENDO OF SILENCE ECHOING AND BOUNDING AROUND THE WALLS AND AIR AROUND US!

AGAIN, THE AIR BECAME UNBEARABLY HOT!

AGAIN, MY LUNGS SEEMED READY TO BURST FOR LACK OF CLEAN COOL FRESH AIR!

AS WE ENTERED INTO A HUGE HIGH CEILINGED CAVERN, THERE WERE SEVERAL WITHERING FORMS ENVELOPED BY AN INFERNO OF WHITE-YELLOW FLAMES,

THE HEAT WAS SO INTENSE, I COULD FEEL MY SKIN BEGINNING TO BLISTER -

BUT AS I LOOKED AT MY ARMS -

ALL WAS WELL!

JESUS LOOKED AT ME, TEARS FLOWING LIKE RIVERS OF IMMENSE AND INTENSE GRIEF -

IN A SOMBER QUITE WHISPER, HE SAID: "DO NOT FRET MY LITTLE ONE -

"NO HARM WILL TOUCH OR COME NEAR YOU!"

"I AM HERE, CLING UNTO ME FOR SAFETY!"

AND SO I CLUNG UNTO MY JESUS, AS THOUGH I WAS A DROWNING SOUL!

I GAZED UPON THE GROTESQUE FORMS OF WHAT ONCE WERE WOMEN -

THEIR BELLIES WERE SO DISTENDED AS THOUGH THEY WERE ABOUT TO GIVE BIRTH!

JESUS EXTENDED HIS ARM, THE FLAMES WERE NO MORE!

"OH! LORD!"

"HELP ME!" THEY ALL SAID IN UNISON.

JESUS, SADLY REPLIED: "OH! MY POOR DELUDED SISTERS!"

"HAVE NOT MY FOLLOWERS STORMED YOUR VERY DOORS OF MURDER!!!

"HAVE NOT MY MANY FOLLOWERS SHOWED YOU THE TRUTH OF YOUR ABOMINABLE SIN!"

"HAVE NOT MY FATHER'S WORDS BEEN SPOKEN TO YOU -

"THAT YOUR BODIES ARE A HOLY TEMPLE -

"NO LUSTFUL DESECRATION BE INFLICTED UPON -

"NO INNOCENT SLAUGHTER OF A NEWBORN LIFE SHOULD BE SNUFFED OUT BECAUSE MY ENEMY IMPLANTED IN YOUR IMAGINATION THAT WITHIN YOU THERE WAS A HORRIBLE PARASITE LIVING AND GROWING FROM YOUR LIFE FORCE!"

ONE SEEMINGLY THE YOUNGEST IN THE GROUP, PITIFULLY CRIED OUT:

"OH! LORD!"

"I DIDN'T KNOW IT WAS A PRECIOUS LIFE!"

"BUT I WAS SO AFRAID OF WHAT MY PARENTS WOULD DO TO ME IF THEY FOUND OUT I WAS PREGNANT!"

ANOTHER JOINED IN, SHE SEEMED TO BE ABOUT MIDDLE AGE, WITH HEAD BOWED DOWN IN SHAME, SHE WHISPERED SOFTLY: "OH! LORD! I HAD FIVE LITTLE ONES ALREADY, WE WERE BARELY SCRAPING A LIVING, I COULDN'T BEAR TO ADD ONE MORE MOUTH TO BE FED! I COULDN'T BEAR THE HARDSHIPS AND SCRIMPING ANY LONGER! I WANTED A BETTER LIFE FOR MY FAMILY! OH! LORD!"

SHE SOBBED SO HEARTBROKENLY!

FINALLY, THE THIRD SPOKE IN A HAUGHTY TONE -

"HOW CAN YOU CALL THAT THING GROWING IN ME - LIFE?"

"IT WAS JUST A FLESHY MASS SWIMMING IN FLUID, JUST LIKE A FISH!"

"BESIDES, IF YOU CREATED US, YOU SHOULD HAVE CREATED BEARING CHILDREN EQUALLY BETWEEN THE SEXES! BUT I CAN SEE WHY YOU DON'T, YOU'RE A MAN,

SO YOU HAVE NO IDEA HOW TRAUMATIZING IT IS TO A

BODY, HOW IMPOSING A SQUEALING BRAT CAN BE!"
AT ONCE THE FLAMES SPRANG UP AND ENGULFED HER!
MOMENTARILY, SHE STOICLY HELD HER PROUDFUL STANCE -
BUT THE FLAMES DEVOURED HUNGRILY AT THE FAST DECOMPOSING BODY!
AMIDST THE FLAMES, SHE PLEADED FOR MERCY!
SOON THE FLAMES ENGULFED THE OTHER TWO, BUT THEIR DISTENDED BELLIES BURST OPEN, AND SPILLED OUT BABY-FORMED GUTS!
"JESUS! LORD! SAVE ME!" THEY WAILED IN UNISON.
THE YOUNGEST ONE BEGGED MY LORD FOR MERCY -
"JESUS, LORD! LET ME GO UP IN THE WORLD!
"LET ME WARN ALL MY FRIENDS NOT TO DO WHAT I DID!"
"PLEASE!"
"GOD!"
"HAVE MERCY ON ME!"
JESUS QUIETLY SPOKE "ITS TOO LATE NOW!"
"HOW CAN THE DEAD SAVE THE DEAD?"
"MY FOLLOWERS WERE ALIVE IN ME, I CALLED YOU NOT TO COMMIT MURDER -
"REMEMBER, MY COMMANDMENT - 'THOU SHALT NOT KILL?"!
"YET, IN YOUR HEART THE DEED WAS DONE!"
"YOUR HEART WAS COLD AND STONY TOWARDS MY FOLLOWERS PLEADING AND INTERCEDING FOR THAT GIFT OF LIFE!"
AS I WITNESSED THIS, I BEGAN SOBBING, MY HEART SHATTERED -
THE ACHE WAS UNBEARABLE! IN A SHAKEN VOICE, I QUIETLY BEGGED JESUS OF NAZARETH, TO TAKE ME AWAY FROM THE PLACE OF DAMNED SOULS!"

SUDDENLY!

FEELING VERY CHILLED TO THE BONE, I ABRUPTLY SAT UP!

WITH FEVERISH EYES, I LOOKED AT MY SURROUNDINGS -

I WAS HOME!

DARKNESS SWALLOWED ME, I FELT THE FINGERS OF FEAR CLUTCHING MY SHATTERED HEART -

BUT THERE IN THE CORNER, MY JESUS GLOWED, BANISHING THE DARKNESS -

YET! -

I COULD NOT LOOK UPON HIM!

WITH FURY BURNING DEEP WITHIN ME -

I SCREAMED AT HIM: "WHY?"

"WHY COULDN'T YOU TAKE THEM OUT OF THAT HELLISH PLACE?"

"WHAT KIND OF GOD ARE YOU, DO YOU TAKE PLEASURE IN TORMENTING US?"

"GO AWAY!" I CRIED OUT IN ANGER AND NOT UNDERSTANDING WHY HE WANTED ME TO SEE SUCH HORROR AND TORMENT!

"JESUS OF NAZARETH!" I CALLED OUT WITH ALL MY HEART!

THERE HE WAS BATHED IN GOLDEN LIGHT -

EYES SO FULL OF PAIN AND TEARS -

I COULD SEE THE WOUNDS ON HIS HANDS -

THEY WERE BLEEDING PROFUSELY!

"JESUS OF NAZARETH!"

"WHY DID YOU TAKE ME ON SUCH A HORRIBLE JOURNEY'!

"IT WAS NOT A JOURNEY OF SORROW!"

"ARE YOU REALLY GOD?"

I KNELT AT HIS FEET, THEY TOO WERE BLEEDING!

I SOBBED AT HIS FEET, MY WHOLE BEING HURTING -

"OH! MY GOD!"

"OH! MY JESUS OF NAZARETH!"

"I'M SORRY FOR INFLICTING EVEN MORE PAIN ON

YOU!"

"FORGIVE ME!"

"HAVE MERCY ON ME, MY LORD!"

"HOW CAN I HELP EASE YOUR SUFFERING?"

I LOOKED UP AT MY SWEET SORROWFUL SAVIOR, AND ALL MY ANGER VANISHED,

AND I SAW JESUS LOOK LIKE THE PICTURE I HAD ON MY NIGHT STAND -

I SAW HIS HEART RINGED WITH A CROWN OF THORNS, WHERE THE THORNS PIERCED HIS HEART, DROPLETS OF CRIMSON BLOOD SPILLED DOWN A WHITE YELLOW TIPPED FLAME SHOT UPWARD IN HIS CHEST -

"MY BELOVED"! HIS VOICE WAS A GENTLE SOOTHING BREEZE, HIS SCENT OF A COUNTRY GARDEN MINGLED WITH PUNGENT AROMATIC SPICES FILLED THE ROOM.

"MY BELOVED, VERILY I SAY, 'GO FORTH TO ALL THE CORNERS OF THIS WORLD,

"SPEAK OF THE HORRORS YOU HAVE SEEN!"

"GO FORTH, SHINE MY FATHER'S GLORY INTO THE GROWING DARKNESS THAT IS FAST DESCENDING, OUR ENEMY IS NOW LOOSED IN FULL MEASURE UPON THIS DYING LAND!

"WHILE IN CAPTIVITY, MANY EVIL SEEDS WERE ALSO PLANTED WITH THE GOOD SEED, THE CHOKING WEEDS ARE FAST MULTIPLYING!"

"GO FORTH, MY BELOVED! SAVE MY FLOCK!"

"THE HOLY COUNSELOR WILL GUIDE YOU AND EMPOWER YOU WITH MY RIGHTEOUS AUTHORITY OF DECLARING AND WAGING VICTORY UPON OUR ENEMY AND HIS MANY EVIL MINIONS!"

"TELL MY SHEEP, MY FLOCK, MY BRIDE, OF MY LOVE!"

TELL MY SHEEP, MY FLOCK, MY BRIDE, OF MY MERCI-FUL COMPASSION!"

"FOR I DO NOT DELIGHT OR CAUSE SORROWS IN THEIR LIVES!"

"FOR I DO NOT DELIGHT SEEING MY ENEMY TOR-

MENTING MY FATHER'S CHILDREN FOR ETERNITY!"
"AND NOW MY BELOVED, I SPEAK PEACE INTO YOUR
SPIRIT, BUT I PIERCE YOUR HEART WITH MY ZEAL OF
LOVE, MERCY, FORGIVENESS, AND COMPASSION
TOWARDS MY FLOCK, MY BRIDE!"
"THUS, I LOVINGLY COMMAND YOU -
"BRING THE LOST, BROKEN, WOUNDED, DELUDED AND
WAYWARD SOULS HOME!"
"BRING TO REPENTANCE AND RESTORATION TO MY
BELOVED BRIDE!"
"DELIVER THE CAPTIVES, TEACH THE REBELLIOUS
LEADERS!"
"HEAL THE SICK AND WOUNDED LITTLE ONES -
"RESURRECT THE DEAD, BRING THEM UNTO EVER-
LASTING LIFE IN AND WITH ME!"
"SPEAK FORTH MY FATHER'S WORDS -
"FOR THEY ARE LIFE!"
"ALL WHO REFUSE TO REPENT AND TURN FROM THEIR
EVIL WORKINGS OF THEIR DARK SECRET CRAFT -
"SHALL RECEIVE THE FULL MEASURE OF MY FATHER'S
WRATH UPON THEM!"
"SPEAK FORTH MY WORDS OF LOVE, JOY, HOPE, PEACE
AND MERCY!"
"SPEAK FORTH MY WORDS OF VICTORY AND FREEDOM
BY THE VICTORY OF CALVARY -
"BY THE FREEDOM THAT BROKE THE ENEMY'S YOKE -
"MY ATONING SHED BLOOD, AS I WAS YOUR PASSOVER
LAMB -
"NOW I AM THE ROARING LION OF THE TRIBE OF
JUDAH -
"LET ALL SEE THE WONDROUS WORKINGS OF MY
HOLY SPIRIT WITHIN YOU AND ALL WHO ABIDE IN ME!
"SPEAK FORTH TO REJOICE - WHEN THE ENEMY TOR-
MENTS AND PERSECUTE YOU FOR MY NAME'S SAKE!"
"SPEAK FORTH TO ALL TO FEAR THE ONE WHO CAN
DESTROY THE BODY AND THE SOUL!"

"TELL ALL -
"COME TO ME ALL YE WHO ARE HEAVILY LADEN!"
"FOR I AM A LIGHT YOKE TO BEAR AND YE BEAR IT NOT ALONE -
"FOR I HAVE GIVEN YOU A GREAT COMMISSION -
"LOVE ONE ANOTHER AS I LOVE YOU -
"BE MY LIGHT TO THIS DARK WORLD AS I AM THE LIGHT, THE WAY, AND THE TRUTH!"
"I LAID MY LIFE DOWN FOR YOU, BELOVED, SO THAT YOU ARE NOW CHILDREN "OF THE MOST HIGH GOD!"
"I AM YOUR DELIVERER, NO LONGER WILL THE ENEMY HAVE AUTHORITY OVER THEE!"
"COME, MY BELOVED BRIDE -
"LET US BE ONE AS MY FATHER AND I ARE ONE -
"COME, MY BELOVED!"

(*Footnote)
Praise the Lord! Jesus needed to set me straight about how to really be born again - I was on 10/28/89, but I still hated the human race, on 4/28/90, and now 7/20/94, as I was typing this, with His revision lesson and impressing my spirit His sword which He really did pierce my heart with, I can look back and understand, God is a spiritual Being, we are carnal - flesh, God's nature isn't ours and our nature isn't His - yet we are created in His image, sin has turned us into a being that is opposite God's. So with Jesus, He became our bridge between the two natures, when He took our sins on Himself, died on the cross, by His sacrifice we really re-became children of the most high God! Praise God!

THE GREAT PROMISE OF
THE LORD FULFILLED

"THE SPIRIT AND THE BRIDE SAY:
"COME, LORD JESUS, COME!!"

"SEE I AM COMING SOON AND MY REWARD IS WITH ME TO REPAY EVERYONE ACCORDING TO THE DEEDS HE HAS DONE.
"I AM THE ALPHA AND OMEGA, THE BEGINNING AND THE END, "THE FIRST AND LAST."
"BLESSED FOREVER ARE ALL WHO ARE WASHING THEIR ROBES,
"TO HAVE THE RIGHT TO ENTER IN THROUGH THE GATES OF THE CITY,
"AND TO EAT THE FRUIT FROM THE TREE OF LIFE."
"YES, I AM COMING SOON!"

(footnote)
From Revelation 22:12-14; Revelation 22:20. Taken from the living Bible.

PRAYER OF SALVATION

"Jesus of Nazareth, I am sorry for the things I have done and said
that was wrong in God's sight.
I believe that you are the Holy Son of God.
I come to you for forgiveness and peace with you, and then with
one another here in this world until you come back for me.
I believe that you died on the cross for my sins, to pay for my sins
that you took my punishment of death so that I can live eternally.
I believe that you were born of a virgin, and rose from the dead.
Please come into my heart.
I give my life to you today. You are my only salvation.
Make me into the person you want me to be.
Take care of me and help me from now on to follow you.
Make me a child of God.

Amen!

A note from the author to the reader of this book.

Please send me a note to let me know that after reading this book, you have decided to trust Jesus of Nazareth as your Lord and Savior and that you have prayed the "Prayer of Salvation."

Thank you so very much for the honor and privilege!
I would like to send you a small gift. Please put down the following information in your note:
Your name, address, city, state, zip code, your age and the date you received our Lord Jesus Christ of Nazareth into your heart!

God Bless and keep you in the shadows of His almighty arms of Love, Grace and Mercy.

Your sister in Christ Jesus of Nazareth -

Lena